IMPROVE YOUR PEOPLE SKILLS

Peter Honey

Institute of Personnel Management

*To James, aged 5, for making such an impressive
start with his people skills.*

© Peter Honey, 1988

First published 1988
Reprinted 1988, 1990, 1992 and 1993

Phototypeset by The Comp-Room, Aylesbury
and printed in Great Britain by
Short Run Press Ltd, Exeter

British Library Cataloguing in Publication Data

Honey, Peter
  Improve your people skills.
  1. Management. Communication
  I. Title
  658.4'5

ISBN 0-85292-396-1

Improve Your People Skills

Dr Peter Honey is a psychologist and management consultant. He worked for Ford Motor Company and British Airways before becoming a freelance in 1969; recent clients include the Automobile Association and the Bank of England, Bass, ICI and Marks and Spencer.

He specializes in anything to do with people's behaviour and its consequences, and divides his time between designing and running training programmes, consultancy assignments and writing. He has written widely on behavioural topics in over fifty publications.

His books include *Developing Interactive Skills*, *Face to Face*, *The Manual of Learning Styles*, *Solving People Problems* and *Solving Your Personal Problems*. He has also written many pamphlets and articles on behavioural topics and featured in the Video Arts production 'Talking about Behaviour'.

He is a Fellow of the Institute of Management Consultants, the Institute of Training and Development and the International Management Centre from Buckingham. He is also a member of the British Psychological Society and the Association for Management Education and Development. He is married, with four children, and lives in Berkshire.

Contents

Contents

Introduction

People skills is a convenient shorthand covering a broad spectrum of different techniques and approaches. There is, however, a common denominator running through all people skills: behaviour. Everything you say and do in your dealings with other people inevitably has an effect on the outcome.

The major difference between you and other people is that you know what you are thinking and feeling, whereas other people only know what you look like and how you are behaving. This fundamental difference between you and everyone else in the world makes your behaviour supremely important.

This book is, therefore, about behaviour; your behaviour in interaction with other people's behaviour. The line taken is that as far as other people are concerned you are your behaviour. In all your dealings with other people your behaviour inevitably plays a major part. It determines the impression they form of you and the way they react to you. Your behaviour is the key ingredient that helps or hinders your relationships with other people.

What follows is written like an encyclopaedia in alphabetical sections that cover all aspects of behaviour. You can choose therefore whether to read it like an ordinary book, from start to finish, or to be selective and only read certain sections. All the sections have been kept short and practical. Most refer you to other sections which are associated or linked in some way.

If you want to be selective here is some guidance on which sections to dip into depending on your starting position.

If you are cynical or sceptical about the importance of behaviour in your dealings with people, the following sections are for you:

Behaviour, pages 13–16
Myths about behaviour, pages 111–113.

If you are already convinced that your behaviour is a key factor in determining your relationships with people but feel unsure about how to enhance your skills, the following sections are for you:

If you frequently experience strong emotion, such as anger or worry, that prevent you from behaving as effectively as you might, the following sections are for you:

If you are beset with people-problems that won't seem to go away, the following section is for you:

If you frequently attend meetings that aren't as productive as you'd wish, the following sections are for you:

If you frequently find yourself in tricky situations where you have to do such things as resolve conflicts, criticize, negotiate, stand your ground, the following sections are for you:

If you simply want straightforward advice on which behaviours to avoid and which to use more often, the following sections are for you:

Introduction

If you read *all* the sections recommended above you would only have read about 20 per cent of the sections on offer. Others examine such things as styles, teamwork, counselling, behaviour on the telephone as well as a host of specific techniques such as asking questions, creative thinking, criticizing, praising, disagreeing, meditating and summarizing.

Inevitably there will be some gaps where you would have welcomed an entry that isn't here. Where this happens please let me know via the publisher and I will be sure to include them in any future revised editions.

Good luck with enhancing your people skills. It amounts to struggling with a whole host of things that are easier said than done and I hope this book encourages you to feel that it is worth the effort.

Acknowledgements

As a self-confessed plagiarist I unreservedly acknowledge all the people who, through things they've said, done or written, have helped me to learn. There are far too many to name but I must at least mention six people who have been major influences.

Ralph Coverdale for introducing me, over 20 years ago, to learning by doing, objective setting and process reviewing; three profound pieces of learning which have endured through all the intervening years and have every appearance of being robust enough to last me for the rest of my life.

Neil Rackham for introducing me to the idea of categorizing behaviour. The emphasis, in various places in this book, on the specificity of behaviour and the way it functions is directly derived from my work with him.

Albert Ellis for rational emotive therapy which succeeded in shifting me from being a hard-nosed behaviourist to being more rounded and embracing emotional feelings in parallel with outward behaviour. His ideas have inspired all the sections in this book that focus on how to prevent unwanted feelings.

B F Skinner for behaviourism. As the undisputed father of behaviourism, all the sections in this book on behaviour change and modification are attributable to him.

Alan Mumford for initially interesting me in the fundamental process of learning from experience and for keeping me abreast with developments in the spheres of learning and management development.

Tony Jay for showing me how to reduce complex behavioural subjects to a few simple, practical messages.

The other major influence has been my wife, Carol, who has given an admirable demonstration of learning and doing in parallel: she mastered the mysteries of a new computer and word processor whilst producing the typescript for this book.

Some of the material which appears in this book inevitably draws on, overlaps with or develops ideas or phrases contained in my earlier publications. I am grateful to the following for allowing me to do so:

Gower Publishing Company Limited, for *Face to Face*

Lloyds of London, for *The Effective Presenter*

McGraw-Hill Book Company, for *Solving People-Problems*

Melrose Films, for 'Teams and Leaders' and 'What the Window Cleaner Saw'

Video Arts, for 'If Looks Could Kill: The Power of Behaviour'; 'Telephone Behaviour: The Power and the Perils' and 'Can You Spare a Moment? The Counselling Interview'.

Peter Honey
Maidenhead

Acquiescence
See *Agreeing* on pages 3–4

Action plans

If you want to modify some aspect of your behaviour, so that you become even more effective in your dealings with people, action plans are vital.

An action plan needs to be *specific* and *feasible*. An action plan with both these characteristics is more likely to get implemented than a plan without them. Indeed a plan without them isn't really a plan at all; it is only an intention. Intentions, however laudable, have a poor track record when it comes to the crunch of implementation. Think of new year resolutions you have made that did not even survive a week.

Here is an example of an unsatisfactory action plan:

I will be more positive

This is flawed because it is too general and not implementable. It is just an intention, not an action plan.

Here is an example of a satisfactory action plan:

Each time I find fault with Bill's ideas I will work out how to improve his idea so that the fault is eased or overcome. I will only allow myself to point out a fault when I have a positive development of his idea to offer. Each stated fault will therefore be matched with a positive suggestion.

This is specific in that it pinpoints exactly when and how I am going to behave positively. It is also feasible because it doesn't unrealistically expect that I am going to be more positive all the time with everyone. The idea is initially to concentrate on being positive in my dealings with Bill and then, when I have been successful with him, to review progress and subsequently plan to extend it, or a version of it, in my dealings with a wider range of people.

Needless to say it makes no sense to have an action plan that doesn't get implemented. Plans have a notorious reputation for needing constant amendment in the light of experience. This is inevitable since the acid test of any plan is how well it works in practice. If it doesn't in the event work out too well then that doesn't mean the plan was useless or that planning is a waste of time. On the contrary, it puts you in a better position to learn from the experience, to review which parts of the plan worked and which didn't and to modify the plan, or scrap it and replace it with another, so that it is more workable. Action planning plays a key part in the process of *learning from experience* (see pages 100–104).

Adaptability

In the course of your life and work you will encounter a wide range of different people: bosses, colleagues, subordinates, customers, suppliers, members of the public, friends, neighbours, relatives, members of your immediate family. People come in all sorts of shapes and sizes, not just in the physical sense but also behaviourally. You'll know people who are friendly and others who are reserved and distant; people who are informal, others who are formal; people who are democratic, others who are autocratic; people who are positive, others who are negative; people who are cheerful, those who are glum and so on.

It follows, therefore, that if you stick rigidly to one fixed behaviour pattern irrespective of whom you are dealing with it will sometimes be inappropriate – one mode of behaviour is not going to be sufficiently compatible with everyone you meet. You need to develop some different behaviour mixes so that you build up a repertoire of different behaviours for different circumstances.

You might find it difficult to accept that this is possible. Many people believe that their behaviour is a fixture rather than a mixture. You may feel that your *personality* (see page 127) sets limits on your behaviour that restrict further adaptability. If you believe this then to some extent you are right. Clearly the sort of person you are, your personality make-up, does put boundaries around you. But, just like the boundaries round a cricket ground, there is considerable scope and room to manoeuvre within those boundaries. The chances are you already adapt your behaviour in different circumstances. For example, when you are amongst friends you probably chatter away quite happily but when you are with strangers you may clam up and have less to say. The fact that you are capable of chattering in one situation and saying less in another already suggests a certain amount of adaptability.

Behaving appropriately is the essence of interpersonal skills. It takes practice to extend your range of behaviours and, having done so, to judge which mix of behaviours to use on which occasion. For further advice on how to do this see *Interpersonal skills* on pages 94–96.

Aggressive behaviour
See *Assertiveness* on pages 8–11

Agreeing

In most conversations there are plenty of behaviours that indicate agreement. The two most obvious are where someone explicitly says they agree and where someone nods their head to signal agreement. But beware! Agreement may be more apparent than real.

The problem is that many people acquiesce and this can easily be mistaken for real agreement. Someone may acquiesce in order to have a quiet life, or because they believe it is 'politic' to fall in line, to 'bend with the wind'. Other people agree because they cannot bear the thought of upsetting someone or because of an overriding desire to be popular.

So it is easy to assume from the way people are behaving that agreement has been reached only to find afterwards that this is not so. This is an important issue when you bear in mind that the objective of most interactions between people is to reach agreement about something or other.

The answer is to guard against assuming agreement and to test for real commitment. Genuinely committed people are likely to do a number of things that leave you in no doubt as to their agreement.

Signs of genuine agreement	*Signs of apparent agreement*
Adding to, embellishing the point	Merely saying yes or not saying no
Volunteering to do something	Holding back and letting other people take on the actions

Enthusiastically identifying benefits of a particular course of action	Deadpan agreements with no sparkle or enthusiasm
Lingering on the point of agreement	Moving on to the next point
Happily committing the agreement to writing	Resisting a written agreement
Accurately and specifically summarizing in own words what has been agreed	Offering no summary or a bland one that avoids specifics
Leaning forward with uncrossed arms and legs	Leaning back with crossed arms and legs
Looking at the other person(s) for at least 50 per cent of the time	Looking down and avoiding direct eye contact

Of course you can never be 100 per cent sure that someone is in genuine agreement until they demonstrate it by doing what they 'agreed' to do. The trick is to *test* for agreement by, for example, inviting the other person to summarize (see *Summarizing* on page 159).

Anger

Anger is an unwanted feeling that frequently spills over into behaviour. It particularly afflicts perfectionists who have such high standards that most people, for most of the time, can't meet them. Fortunately anger is a preventable feeling but it is vital to read the section on *Preventing unwanted feelings* (on page 138) before reading the remainder of this section because what follows assumes that you have understood the two options involved.

Unproductive anger hinders your behaviour in a variety of ways. All or some of the following might apply to you:

- You temporarily suspend rational thinking and say or do insane/ exaggerated things.
- You shout, rant, rave, swear.

Anger

- You physically hit out at objects or people.
- You get yourself into indefensible corners by making absurd threats ('I'll fire you.' 'I'll never speak to you again.') or by saying things which are untrue ('I hate you.' 'I never want to see you again.') or by laying down dogmatic ultimatums ('Never let me catch you doing that again.').
- You make mountains out of molehills.

Your anger is always triggered by some external event or happening. Typical examples might be when:

- you are thwarted by people who do not measure up to your high standards (they don't do what you expected or what they promised to do).
- you are frustrated by obstacles such as being kept waiting, finding a vital shop is shut, being stuck in a traffic jam, making an unforced error in a highly competitive game etc.
- you discover you have been tricked or exploited or have suffered an injustice.
- someone insults you or someone close/important to you.
- faced with circumstances that are not going the way you would like them to.
- inanimate objects 'misbehave' (hammers that hit you instead of the nail, rusty bolts that will not budge, misplaced things that refuse to be found etc.)

Clearly, ideas for changing the events that trigger your anger will depend on the exact circumstances, but here are some thought-starters that might help you to arrive at a feasible plan:

- Keep a log on people/events that trigger your anger. Then plan to avoid or minimize your exposure to them.
- Hand pick people who measure up to your high standards/do things 'your way'. Surround yourself with 'yes' people.
- Check that people understand what you want from them and check on progress well before the final deadline.
- Minimize the frustration of unavoidable obstacles such as being kept waiting/stuck in a traffic jam by having contingency plans (a good book to read, a piece of work to get on with etc.)
- Stick to circumstances/situations where you have a reasonable chance of controlling the way things turn out.

Rather than modify anything to do with the external events that trigger your anger you might decide to go for option 2 and identify the thoughts or beliefs that herald your anger and examine them for possible replacements. Typical thoughts for feelings of anger are:

- They are wrong and I am right.
- Things are not the way they should/ought to be.
- They are making a mess of it – I must put them right.
- They are incompetent fools – they deserve what's coming!
- How dare they do this to me!
- They have no right to be doing this to me!
- This is serious.
- He/she is *making* me angry.
- Anyone would be angry in these circumstances – it's only natural!

And, finally, here are some thought-starters on ways of replacing unrealistic thoughts and beliefs that provoke feelings of anger so that they become more realistic and less likely to hinder your behaviour:

- I wouldn't have done it that way myself.
- I'm disappointed things weren't going the way I had hoped but it isn't worth getting angry about.
- Nothing is important enough to get angry about.
- They have a right to do it their own way.
- I'm annoyed/disappointed/irritated but not angry.
- Nothing can *make* me angry. I decide whether to be angry or not.
- I wonder why they are doing it that way?
- This is funny! (as opposed to serious).
- Count to 20 – slowly!

Appearance
See *First impressions* on pages 69–70

Appraisals

Appraisals, done properly, are an honest attempt to appraise some-one's current performance (ie behaviour) and to help them identify how to improve. Unfortunately appraisals are rarely done frequently enough or properly and so they finish up having a bad reputation both with appraisers and appraisees.

Formal appraisal systems were invented to force appraiser and appraisee to do an appraisal at least once per year. The system usually puts the onus of responsibility on the appraiser. Appraisals work far better, however, when the appraisee takes the initiative and is determined to use the occasion as an opportunity to solicit feedback (see *Feedback* on page 63). If the appraisee wants to learn (see *Learning from experience* on page 100), has a clear objective for the appraisal (see *Objectives* on page 119) and has the behavioural skills to extract help, then appraisals happen more frequently and are more useful. The key skills for getting help are:

- asking for feedback on current performance.
- asking for 'evidence', examples, illustrations, actual incidents.
- accepting the information for what it is; the other person's *perception* of your performance.
- asking for ideas on how current performance can be improved.
- reacting to ideas by building on them rather than resisting them.

The behaviours that wreck the process of getting help are:

- being defensive and justifying why you did the things under discussion.
- failing to ask for specific examples.
- trying to convince the other person that they are wrong.
- explaining why an idea isn't practicable, acceptable.

The key to successful appraisals, as with most other interactions in life, is to behave appropriately.

Asking questions

Asking questions of one sort or another accounts for at least 25 per cent of most conversations. There are questions:

- to get ideas ('How could we solve that?')
- to get a reaction to ideas ('What do you think of that?')
- to check whether someone is in agreement ('Do you agree?')
- to clarify something ('Do you mean . . . ?')
- to get information ('What is today's date?')
- to get opinions ('What views do you hold on capital punishment?')
- to find out somebody's needs ('What colour would you prefer?')
- to identify a problem ('How often does he do that?') and so on.

Questions demand answers and in that sense they are a good example of the power of behaviour. If you ask someone a question, nine times out of ten you will be successful in getting an appropriate answer. Asking questions is the key to being a good conversationalist. If you question people in a way that invites them to open-up and be expansionist invariably they will enjoy the experience and think well of you.

Open-ended questions are more fruitful than closed-ended ones. Open questions avoid yes-no answers and begin with what, when, where, how and who. If you ask someone 'Do you travel to work by train?', it only requires them to answer 'yes' or 'no' as the case may be. If you ask 'How do you travel to work?', it requires them to be more forthcoming. Open-ended questions are especially useful in getting silent and/or sullen people to open-up.

Assertiveness

Assertiveness is the label given to a collection of behaviours that stem from a belief that your needs or wants are as important as other people's. The alternatives are to believe that your needs or wants are *less* or *more* important than other people's. The former results in submissive behaviour, the latter in aggressive behaviour.

People oscillate between the three modes of behaviour depending on circumstances. Most people, however, when faced with a tricky situation tend to react aggressively or submissively rather than assertively, despite the fact that assertive behaviour is more likely to lead to a resolution that is satisfactory to all concerned (see *Win-win* on page 174).

Assertive behaviour

is when you
- stand up for your own rights in a way that does not violate another person's rights.

It leads to an honest, open and direct expression of your point of view which, at the same time, shows that you understand the other person's position.

Submissive behaviour

is when you
- fail to stand up for your rights or do so in such a way that others can easily disregard them.
- express your thoughts, feelings and beliefs in apologetic, cautious or self-effacing ways.
- fail to express your views or feelings altogether.

Submission is based on the belief that your own needs and wants will be regarded by others as relatively unimportant. Typical of submissive behaviour are long, justifying, self-deprecating explanations and ingratiating attempts to accommodate the needs and wants of other people.

Aggressive behaviour

is when you
- stand up for your own rights in such a way that you violate the rights of another person.
- express thoughts, feelings and beliefs in unsuitable and inappropriate ways, even though you may honestly believe those

views to be right.

Aggression is based on the belief that your opinions are more important than other people's. It is characterized by accusing and blaming other people, showing contempt, and by being hostile or patronizing.

Examples of each mode of behaviour

Suppose Christmas is approaching and you are asked to take on some extra duties because of the rush. In a way, it is an honour to be asked but it will mean working changed shifts and probably some extra ones, too. You are already fully committed and feeling stretched and overworked. Here are three answers you might give in reply to the request:

An assertive answer:

'I quite understand that you need these jobs done, but I don't see how I can fit them in at the moment. I would like to help, so can we look at some alternative ways of tackling them?'

A submissive answer:

'Well, I don't really have any spare time at the moment, but I suppose I could fit it all in. I'll manage to rearrange something, I expect, er . . . OK, I don't mind.'

An aggressive answer:

'You must be joking! Just before Christmas? I'm up to my ears already! There's no way I'll manage that as well. You'll have to find somebody else.'

Let's look more closely at the actual words or phrases people are likely to use when being assertive, submissive or aggressive.

People behaving assertively are likely to:

● Make statements that are brief and to the point.
● Use 'I' statements, eg I think, I believe, I'd like, I want, I need.

- Distinguish clearly between fact and opinion, eg In my experience . . . My opinion is . . . As I see it . . .
- Avoid words like, You should . . . , You ought . . .
- Use open-ended questions to find out the thoughts, opinions, wants of others, eg How does this affect you? What are your thoughts on . . . ?
- Look for ways to resolve problems, eg How can we get around that? How about . . . ?

People behaving submissively are likely to:

- Make long rambling statements (often justifying themselves).
- Avoid making 'I' statements, or qualify them, eg It's only my opinion but . . .
- Use other qualifying phrases or words, eg Maybe . . . Would you mind very much . . . I wonder if . . . Just . . . Sorry to bother you but . . .
- Use 'filler' words, eg Uh . . . You know . . . , Sort of . . .
- Put themselves down, eg I seem to be hopeless at this. I can't . . .
- Use phrases which make it easier for others to ignore their needs or wants, eg It's not important really. It doesn't matter.

People behaving aggressively are likely to:

- Make excessive use of 'I' statements.
- State their opinions as facts, eg That approach won't work. That's rubbish.
- Use threats, eg You'd better do it.
- Put others down, eg You must be joking. That's only *your* opinion. You cannot be serious.
- Make a lot of use of the words 'ought', 'must', 'should' and 'have to'.
- Be keen to attach blame to others, eg It was *your* fault. Well, I blame *you*.

Since behaviour breeds behaviour, assertive behaviour is more likely to trigger assertive behaviour in other people and thus lead to a better outcome. If you tend to be submissive in *tricky situations* (see page 168) then you need to beef yourself up by practising the assertive behaviours. If, on the other hand, you are inclined to be aggressive in tricky situations then you need to tone yourself down by practising the assertive behaviours.

Assumptions

Assumptions are inevitable because you can never have *all* the facts. When you plan a meeting with someone, for example, it is inevitable that you will assume that you are both still alive, that the meeting will take place, that the other person will wear clothes, that they will speak and so on. These are examples of assumptions it is worth making since the likelihood of them happening is extremely high. There are other assumptions which are less reliable, however. For example, you might assume in your preparations that the person already knows certain things or that the person will take up a certain position. Your objectives are likely to be inappropriate and your plan is likely to flounder if neither of these assumptions is in fact the case.

The real danger with assumptions is when you fail to distinguish between them and hard, factual data. If you forget that an assumption is only an assumption, then you are vulnerable and likely to have all sorts of nasty surprises. If you assume, for example, that someone is reliable and will do what they said they'd do, you are unlikely to think it necessary to check. Failure to take this simple precaution may mean that you in turn will be unreliable because you were dependent on the other person who let you down.

So assumptions are fine providing you don't start taking them for granted. When an assumption starts to become a belief (see *Beliefs* on page 21), it is time to remind yourself that assumptions are only assumptions and only safe when recognized as such.

Attitudes

Attitudes are recurring thoughts and beliefs that predispose you to react (ie behave) in certain ways. If, for example, you believe that all psychologists are 'weirdos', that all trade unionists are militants and that all children are a nuisance, then these attitudes are likely to affect your behaviour whenever you come into contact with psychologists, trade unionists and children.

Attitudes have a lot to answer for. Whenever there is a problem with the way people are behaving attitudes tend to get blamed as the villain of the piece. Attempts to change people's attitudes are incredibly hit and miss and generally speaking have a poor track record of success. Broadly there are two lines of attack:

1 Persuasion (see *Persuasiveness* on page 128) where attempts are made to reason with people and show them it is in their interest to change their attitude. The assumption here is that a changed attitude will automatically result in a changed behaviour, ie that the underlying attitude *caused* the outward behaviour.

2 The introduction of inducements of various kinds to 'force' a behaviour change. This can be done by making external changes to the situation in which the behaviour is occurring. If, for example, people are found to make fewer mistakes when the lights are bright then you introduce brighter lights and save your breath when it comes to persuading people to be more quality conscious. The assumption here is that a changed environment will automatically result in a changed behaviour, ie that the external environment caused the outward behaviour. Attitudes are left to their own devices.

Which approach is best? My answer is the second one because actions speak louder than words and because it seems daft to take an indirect approach, ie via attitudes, when a direct one will do the trick. Notice, however, that the two approaches are not exclusive. You can use both in parallel: a propaganda campaign aimed at changing attitudes together with a rejigging of the environment aimed at changing behaviour.

Behaviour

You have probably been told to 'behave yourself' and 'be on your best behaviour' hundreds of times, if not recently then certainly when you were a child. This tends to give behaviour moralistic undertones as to whether it is good or bad, right or wrong, acceptable or unacceptable.

In this book, however, I am using the word behaviour in its 'pure' sense to refer to any overt, or obvious, action. Overt actions are plain to see and include everything we say to people as well as non-verbal movements such as facial expressions, gestures with hands and arms, and 'body language' in general. Behaviour is smiling, frowning, shaking someone's hand, giving someone 'two fingers', looking at someone when they are talking, doodling, agreeing, disagreeing, shouting, whispering, praising, criticizing – everything. Literally all you do and anyone else does is behaviour.

The main point to grasp is that behaviour is always directly observable, unlike many accompanying underlying factors, such as motives, attitudes, beliefs and emotional feelings, which are all covert and never directly observable.

Behaviour, therefore, is rather like the tip of an iceberg.

The way you behave is important because:

• The conclusions you reach about other people (ie whether you like or dislike them, trust or distrust them) are based solely on the way you see them behave (ie their actions both spoken and unspoken).
• The conclusions other people reach about you are based on the only part of you they have ready access to – your behaviour.
• In person to person relationships nothing is more important than behaviour. Judgements *have* to be based on it.
• Since your behaviour is so evident in a person to person encounter it influences (shapes) the other person's behaviour and *vice versa*. You can only modify other people's behaviour and attitudes through your own.

Your behaviour is, therefore, a tool which you can use to help or hinder your dealings with other people. Consider the following five examples:

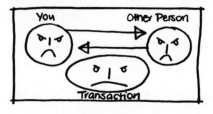

Your behaviour affects the other person for the worse.

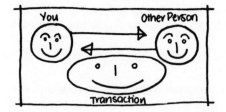

Your behaviour affects the other person for the better.

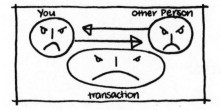

You let the other person's behaviour affect you for the worse.

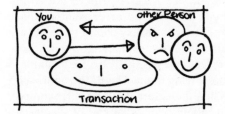

You did not let the other person's behaviour affect you for the worse and succeeded in using your behaviour to affect the other person for the better.

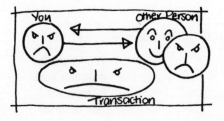

You did not let the other person's behaviour affect you for the better and even succeeded in affecting the other person for the worse.

An implication in all this is that you can change your behaviour and, via that, other people's behaviour. Since you have learned to behave the way you do now, through an *ad hoc* process of learning from experience, there is no reason why you shouldn't unlearn and relearn.

When it comes to developing your own behavioural skills the following is good advice:

- Put your behaviour first and your underlying attitudes and feelings second, ie smile in order to feel happy rather than smiling when you feel happy.
- Set yourself specific behaviour targets and plan to expand your repertoire of behaviour.
- Force yourself to behave appropriately until you have acquired the behaviour in question and no longer need consciously to force it.

Behaviour modification

Behaviour modification (BMod) is the name given to a problem solving approach that specializes in solving people problems. People problems occur when the behaviour you have got from someone is not the behaviour you want. Suppose, for example, that someone with whom you have frequent dealings tends to be negative (ie pointing out snags and difficulties, explaining why it won't work) and you want them to react more positively by, for example, improving ideas rather than destroying them. The BMod approach comes to the rescue by analysing the external events surrounding the behaviour in question and identifying what can be changed. Briefly the problem solving approach is based on the following model:

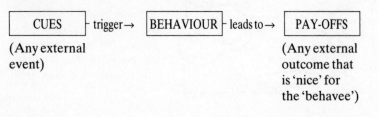

The approach invites you to identify 'problem' behaviours (such as resistance to change, aggressiveness, procrastination) together with their surrounding external events (cues and pay-offs). The problem is then solved by working out how to change the cues and/or pay-offs. BMod is effective in tackling entrenched behavioural tendencies which have resisted change by persuasion or counselling or training.

Returning to the example of the negative person, what sort of external events might be triggering negative behaviour? To identify the cues that are triggering this behaviour we need to ask ourselves, 'What is it that occurs just before someone explains why things can't be done?' The answer to this question will give us some likely cues. Typical answers might be that:

- suggestions for change come 'out of the blue';
- he or she is presented with a *fait accompli* with no consultation along the way;
- the suggestion is put to him or her in a meeting with subordinates present.

We can now look at ways of changing such cues. Alternatively, we can consider what happens *after* the behaviour that is an encouraging consequence or outcome for the person.

So, in the case of the negative person, we need to ask: 'What is it that happens after he or she has explained why things can't be done that counts as a satisfactory outcome (pay-off)?' Answers to this question might be:

- on a high percentage of occasions resistance wins the day (causes the proposed changes to be dropped or significantly lessened);
- the proposers pay attention to him or her;
- people congratulate him or her for being a stickler;
- it avoids (or minimizes) the need to make changes;
- it creates a situation where he or she can say 'If things go wrong, don't blame me. I've warned you';
- subordinates show that they admire the way he or she protects/ represents them.

Now we have the whole picture. We can see, much as we may not welcome it, why the person is negative – not only is the behaviour triggered by certain events, it is also clear that it is very advantageous to the negative person. There is every advantage in behaving in this way. In short, the behaviour results in pay-offs for our negative person and, while this state of affairs continues, so will the negative behaviour. As surely as babies cry for attention, he or she will react negatively when people propose changes.

So what is to be done about it? We might, of course, decide that the negative points were valid and useful and therefore decide to grin and bear it. On the other hand, we might see considerable advantage in getting him or her to convert the negative behaviour into something more positive by, for example, putting effort into suggesting improvements to the ideas. We could do this by changing the cues so that he or she is consulted on a person-to-person basis rather than presented with *faits accomplis*. Now we have something to work on at the other end, after the behaviour has occurred. The pay-offs give us a whole host of possible actions.

For example, the discovery that resistance wins the day and causes proposed changes to be dropped or lessened means that we could be careful to ensure that this outcome only occurs when he or she has been positive and not negative. This would be a reversal of the current state of affairs. When the person is negative there are no concessions; it is only when he or she is less negative that there is a pay-off. This means that, for suggesting modifications to the proposed changes, the reward is winning the day. Blocking any modifications, on the other hand, means losing the day.

If this reversal of the usual pattern of events is repeated on a number of occasions, we would expect to see the person become less negative and more positive in the face of change. If you couple this pay-off strategy with the ideas we had earlier about altering the cues, then it is very likely indeed that the problem of negative behaviour will be overcome. The combination of cues and pay-offs is enormously potent. The altered cues make it less likely that the negative behaviour will occur in the first place; when it does, the altered pay-offs ensure that there is no longer any advantage in it. Quite the reverse, in fact; there is now every advantage in being positive.

The other pay-offs we listed could be built into the strategy in a similar way; they all have a contribution to make. For example, one pay-off that resulted from negative behaviour was increased attention from the proposers. In future, they would need to be careful to pay more attention when the person was positive and less when he or she was negative. Another pay-off was congratulations for being a stickler. Well, now it must be arranged so that the congratulations come only for *improving* the proposed changes.

The BMod approach can be reduced to seven simple steps:
1 Be clear and specific about the problem behaviour.
2 Identify the cues that trigger the behaviour.
3 Identify the pay-offs the behaviour results in.
4 Decide what behaviour you want.
5 Work out how to change the cues.
6 Work out how to use the pay-offs to encourage the wanted behaviour.
7 Check for feasibility and implement.

Behaviourism

The behaviourist is in business to control and predict behaviour by modifying the connections between external events and observable behaviour. The hallmarks of a behaviourist approach are:

- It focuses on actual, overt, manifest reactions (behaviour).
- It pinpoints links between behaviour and its preceding and following external events.
- It focuses exclusively on current, 'here and now' behaviours and external events.
- It thrives on specificity.

The main distinction between behaviourism and other approaches is, therefore, the emphasis it places on the external causes of behaviour. By contrast other approaches tend to regard behaviour as a symptom and to focus on internal causes such as underlying needs, motives, attitudes and feelings. An 'internalist' is assertive because he feels confident, whereas a behaviourist is assertive in order to be confident.

Behaviourism has three obvious benefits:
1 The advantage of putting behaviour itself in the spotlight is that it helps us to understand that, whether we like it or not, our behaviour is the part of us that has the most impact on other people (and therefore on how they react to us). Behaviourists

find it easy to accept that their overt behaviour is the key factor in determining their relationships with people. Accordingly, when behaviourists have trouble with other people's behaviour they ask themselves, 'What is it that I am doing to trigger that reaction?'

2 The advantage of concentrating on the connections between external events, both preceding and ensuing, and behaviour is that it is much more straightforward than speculating about the links between internal events and behaviour. If, for example, I observe that David keeps interrupting me it is relatively straightforward to identify when he interrupts me (whenever I disagree with him) and what ensues after he has interrupted me (I stop disagreeing with him). Internalists, on the other hand, have a more complex analysis to explain why David keeps interrupting me. This is because they are dealing with intangible factors rather than a sequence of tangible events. Internalists are therefore left speculating about David's motives (he wants to put you down in front of your mutual boss), or attitudes (he hates bearded psychologists), or feelings (he is feeling threatened). The behaviourist's explanation of any piece of behaviour is always more straightforward than the internalist's.

3 Finally the behaviourist's approach is more practical than any alternative I have ever come across. It is practical because it deals in specifics rather than platitudinous generalizations and concentrates on the here and now, rather than tracing behaviour back to its historical origins ('He is feeling threatened and therefore interrupting you because his mother used to interrupt him when he was sitting on his potty'). Hand in hand with the simplicity of the behaviourist's explanation goes an appealing practicality. If David interrupts me when I disagree with him, and if I want to modify his behaviour then I must look to my own, either by no longer disagreeing or by finding a more fruitful way to do it (for example, by giving a reason before I say I am in disagreement). This is utterly practical and since I am modifying tangible events I will get immediate feedback about the success or failure of my strategy.

So behaviourism offers simple, practical explanations for behaviour. It does not pretend to be the full story but enough of it for practical purposes. Behaviourists do not deny either the existence or the influence of the internal causes of behaviour. They merely want to get full utilization out of the external causes before complicating the issue. It is this that appeals to the busy practising manager who has previously been baffled by internal explanations of behaviour leaving him short of techniques that he can use on a day-to-day basis.

Beliefs

Beliefs are rather like *Attitudes* (see page 12) in that they are internal recurring thoughts that obviously have a significant influence on how people react (ie behave). Beliefs are, in effect, conclusions that you have reached based on experience. They are often deep-seated (which is why they tend to recur) and not necessarily rational in the sense that they often fail to stand up to close scrutiny or to match 'the facts'.

Beliefs have a tendency to be self-reinforcing. If, for example, you believe that all redheads are short-tempered, then you tend to sustain that belief despite the fact that most of the redheads you have dealings with are no more short-tempered than anyone else. If you were unfortunate enough to meet a redhead who *was* short-tempered, then you would seize on that as 'proof' and conveniently forget all the redheads who had failed to match the belief.

Beliefs are useful because they are a short cut. Without them we would have to process all the data and come to a carefully considered conclusion every time in every situation and this would be onerous as well as time-consuming. The problem with beliefs, however, is that they are often:

- behind the times
- dogmatic and absolute
- unrealistic.

The combined effect of these characteristics is often most unfortunate. Whenever you get upset and agitated, for example, it is because a belief you hold dear has been violated. Suppose you believe that people *ought* always to be polite. (The ought is significant. Beliefs are usually in the form of oughts, shoulds and musts.) Armed with this belief you are clearly vulnerable when, as will inevitably happen from time to time, someone is rude to you. The occurrence of rudeness is in direct contradiction to your belief that people ought always to be polite. This causes you to get upset to such an extent that you might even match rudeness with rudeness and therefore escalate the situation.

The solution is to break the vicious circle and instead of retaining unrealistic beliefs, and therefore getting upset whenever they are violated, subject the belief itself to scrutiny and modify it to something more reasonable. This is the key to *preventing unwanted feelings* (see page 138). Here, to whet your appetite, are some typical unrealistic beliefs and beside each a more realistic version:

Unrealistic beliefs	*Realistic beliefs*
I need/*must* have everyone's approval	I like approval/want it but at least 50 per cent of the people I meet probably won't approve of me
People *should* always be competent and do things perfectly	People are fallible and sometimes make mistakes
People *ought* not to be wicked and evil. They *should* be nice, fair, just, honest, etc etc	Some people, for some of the time, behave in unacceptable ways. It is preferable when they are nice, fair, just, honest, etc etc
I *ought* to feel upset when things go wrong	I can choose how I feel, even when things go wrong
External events *make* me feel angry, worried, guilty, happy, etc etc	I am responsible for deciding whether or not to feel angry, worried, guilty, happy, etc etc
I *ought* to worry about dangerous things that might happen	Dangerous things will inevitably happen from time to time. (There is a vast difference between worrying about something which may never happen and taking sensible precautions in case something does happen.)
Things *ought* to go the way I want them to	I prefer it when things go the way I want them to

For further advice about how to set about converting an unrealistic belief to a realistic one see *Preventing unwanted feelings* on pages 138–141.

Boredom

Boredom is an unwanted feeling that frequently spills over into behaviour. Fortunately boredom is a preventable feeling but it is vital to read the section on *Preventing unwanted feelings* (on page 138) before reading the remainder of this section because what follows assumes you have understood the two options involved.

Unproductive boredom hinders your behaviour in a variety of ways. All or some of the following might apply to you:

- You stop paying attention/switch off/yawn/doodle/rock/eat or drink too much.
- You waste time mooning around not taking any initiatives.
- You linger (hoping things will improve) when you should go.
- You blame/condemn other people for boring you.
- You indulge in ill-considered pranks/ploys to counteract the boredom.

Your boredom is always triggered by some external event or happening. Typical examples might be when:

- listening to repetitive, drawn-out talks/attending meetings.
- passively spectating while other people are active.
- you are compelled to kill time waiting (ie in queues, waiting rooms, at airports, railway stations etc).
- doing routine, repetitive manual tasks that you have done hundreds of times before.
- you have spent too long at any one activity, whatever it is.
- talking to people who talk exclusively *at* you about themselves and never enquire about you or solicit your views.

Clearly, ideas for changing the events that trigger your boredom will depend on the exact circumstances, but here are some thought-starters that might help you to arrive at a feasible plan:

- Keep a log on people/events that trigger your boredom. Then

plan to avoid or minimize your exposure to them.
- At talks/meetings ask lots of questions.
- Don't watch people doing things – join in.
- Spend no longer than 30 minutes doing any one activity. Intersperse it with something contrasting (ie if you have been engaged in a thinking activity do a physical one next or *vice versa*).
- Become your own work study expert. Analyse how you do repetitive tasks and think of different permutations/more effective methods.
- At meetings/concerts/in waiting rooms set yourself interesting challenges – study people's faces, memorize all the objects in the room, invent metaphors, count the number of times people say 'you know', study non-verbal gestures, write a poem/description of what it feels like to be bored, pretend you are a newspaper reporter writing a gripping piece on the event etc.
- Get up and go.

Rather than modify anything to do with the external events that trigger your boredom you might decide to go for option 2 and identify the thoughts or beliefs that herald your boredom and examine them for possible replacements. Typical thoughts for feelings of boredom are:

- This is boring me.
- He/she is boring me.
- I wish I was doing something else.
- What a waste of time – but I'd better hang on in case it gets better/ I miss something.

And, finally, here are some thought-starters on ways of replacing unrealistic thoughts and beliefs that provoke feelings of boredom so that they become more realistic and less likely to hinder your behaviour:

- In half an hour I may be dead – I'm *damned* if I'm going to spend it feeling bored!
- Nothing is boring – it's just that I sometimes choose to feel bored.
- 'The man who lets himself be bored is even more contemptible than the bore' (Samuel Butler).

Brainstorming

See *Creative thinking* on pages 41–44.

Building

Building is a relatively rare behaviour. In a typical problem-solving discussion it only represents three per cent of all the spoken behaviours. Interactively-skilled people tend to push this up to eight per cent.

Building behaviour occurs when someone develops, or adds to, *someone else's* idea. If, for example, someone said: 'How about negotiating a new completion date?', someone could build on it by saying: 'Now there's an idea and we could sugar the pill by offering to extend our follow-up service by an extra six months.'

Building is a rare species because:

- people often don't listen sufficiently carefully to other people's ideas. If you haven't heard the idea you are not in a position to build upon it.
- even if people have heard the idea they are likely to find it easier to analyse it than to develop it. Ideas (especially other people's ideas) can easily be analysed to death. (See *Difficulty stating* on page 52).
- people are often competitive and an idea from someone else becomes a challenge, not to develop it, but to produce a better alternative. 'I didn't get where I am today by developing other people's ideas!'
- people often find it difficult to think on their feet and react there and then to an idea from someone else. Building doesn't *have* to happen immediately but often the opportunity is missed and the moment passes if it doesn't happen soon after the idea was first mooted.

The best way to become a builder rather than a destroyer is to practise the following routine.

1 When someone suggests an idea (ie a possible course of action)
   listen to it without interrupting.
2 Check that you have understood it correctly by summarizing it
   back in your own words.
3 Think to yourself 'What is wrong with the idea?' but don't *say* it.
4 Make it a rule that you will only permit yourself to express your
   concerns when you have something constructive to add to the
   idea.

Most ideas are capable of development. If you come across an idea
that really stumps you, the best plan is to state your concerns and
invite other people to have a crack at building.

Categories of behaviour

People often express unease with labelling or pigeon-holing human
behaviour. There is, however, no alternative. The only way to
make sense of behaviour is to break it down into some specifics.
Every science adopts a category system and the behavioural sciences
are no exception.

The advantage of using categories is that otherwise vague, global
notions of behavioural differences between people can be pinpointed more precisely. This clarity helps both when observing
other people's behaviour (we are less likely to succumb to the perils
of jumping to a conclusion) and when planning how best to behave
ourselves.

Behaviour, in common with everything else, is capable of
description at different levels. There are personality-level descriptions such as extrovert and introvert. There are style-level
descriptions such as autocratic and democratic. There are role-level
descriptions such as leader, doer, thinker, supporter. Behaviour-
level descriptions complement all these by breaking them down
into smaller units (in rather the same way that Eskimos have over
50 categories to distinguish between different types of snow). Thus
an autocratic style, on closer analysis, breaks down into a number
of behaviours including:

- Telling rather than asking
- Proposing, instructing, commanding
- Interrupting, cutting people off
- Disagreeing.

A democratic style, on the other hand, breaks down into some of the following behaviours:

- Asking, rather than telling
- Suggesting
- Listening, summarizing back
- Agreeing and checking that others agree.

For convenience, *verbal behaviour* (see page 170) can be broken down into nine categories as follows:

Seeking ideas	Asking other people for their ideas.
Proposing	Putting forward ideas (possible courses of action) as statements.
Suggesting	Putting forward ideas as questions (ie 'How about doing so and so')
Building	Developing someone else's idea.
Disagreeing	Explicitly disagreeing with something someone else has said.
Supporting	Agreeing with something someone else has said.
Difficulty stating	Pointing out the snags or difficulties with something someone else has said.
Seeking clarification/ information	Asking other people for further clarification or information.
Clarifying/explaining/ informing	Giving information, opinions and explanations.

Non-verbal behaviour (see page 116) also has a category system which breaks down all the visual behaviours into:

- facial expressions
- eyes
- hand movements

- gestures with hands and arms
- leg movements
- body posture
- spatial distance and orientation.

There is nothing sacrosanct about any of these categories. They can be expanded or reduced depending on purpose and context. Behaviour categories are invaluable when it comes to planning appropriate behaviour (see *Planning behaviour* on page 131).

Chairing meetings

Chairing a meeting is a full-time job. Getting involved in the subject matter of a meeting and chairing it are two roles that do not mix. Successful chairing is greatly aided by being uninvolved, disinterested and impartial. It is precisely because these are such difficult behaviours to adopt that most people fail to match up to the requirements of the job.

The basic functions of a chairperson are well-known (but that doesn't necessarily mean they are well done). It is the chair's responsibility to:

- start the meeting by clarifying the objectives and checking that all participants have a shared understanding;
- introduce each topic (the 'what') briefly by putting it into context and explaining the purpose/objective (the 'how') by either suggesting or gathering ideas from participants;
- control the pace of the meeting by agreeing a time slot for each topic and checking progress against the time plan;
- control the flow of conversation by restraining the verbose and bringing in quieter participants;
- keep the discussion to the point by summing up at frequent intervals and by asking questions of clarification;
- conclude each topic by summarizing what has been agreed or decided;
- conclude the meeting by recapping the actions that have been placed on people and checking that all participants have a shared understanding of each action;
- review whether or not the meeting was successful in achieving

the objectives by gathering ideas on what went well and what could have gone better.

In a nutshell, the chairperson's role is to facilitate the meeting by being custodian of the processes rather than contributing directly to the topics themselves.

For more advice on how to chair effectively see *Meetings*, pages 106–109, and *Groups*, pages 77–80.

Change

All change inevitably involves behaviour change. Despite the fact that it is popular to talk about changing attitudes, in the last analysis it is always behaviour that needs to change. If someone changed their attitudes but not their behaviour that would be deemed a failure. If, on the other hand, someone changed their behaviour in the required direction then, regardless of whether this was accompanied by an attitudinal change or not, it would be hailed as a success.

Changing behaviour is always an uphill struggle because, quite understandably, people prefer the convenience of sticking to the behaviour patterns they have come to know and love rather than the inconvenience and upheaval of switching to behaviours that are new and unfamiliar. For this reason, changes always provoke some form of human resistance (see *Resistance to change*, page 145).

There are four alternative strategies for introducing change. The key to success is to use a strategy, or combination of strategies, appropriate to the type of resistance.

Negotiate

If the resistance stems from parochial self-interest, ie people are going to lose something of value as a result of the change, then the best strategy is to negotiate by offering incentives to the resisters or potential resisters.

Educate

If the resistance stems from misunderstandings or lack of trust, ie

people through ignorance *imagine* they are going to lose something
of value as a result of the change, then the best strategy is to educate
by communicating the reasons for, and benefits of, the change.

An education programme works best where there is a good
relationship between the initiators and resisters, otherwise the latter may not believe what they hear.

Participate

If the resistance stems from different assessments, ie people have
different perceptions of the changes that are necessary, then the
best strategy is to involve the resisters, or potential resisters, in
some form of participative programme. Involving others makes
very good sense when the initiators of change recognize that they
do not have all the information and/or that they need the
wholehearted support of others to design and implement the
change. Considerable research has shown that participation leads
to commitment, not just compliance.

Force and support

If the resistance stems from a low tolerance for change, ie people
are fearful that they will not be able to cope, then the best strategy
is to force the change through and support and reinforce the resultant
new behaviours. This strategy needs more explanation than the
previous three.

The argument in favour of this strategy is rather similar to those
in support of legislation that is designed to force people to change
their ways and thus learn new patterns of behaviour. Legislation of
this kind is always controversial (examples are racial and sexual
discrimination, legislation to force motorcyclists to wear helmets,
motorists to wear seat belts and so on) since they explicitly coerce
people into changing regardless of protests and appeals to 'free
will'. Coercion gambles that the forced change will put people in a
situation where they will eventually come to terms with the change.
The following simplification shows the vicious circle that coercion
seeks to break.

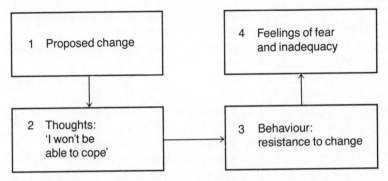

By contrast the force/support strategy looks like this:

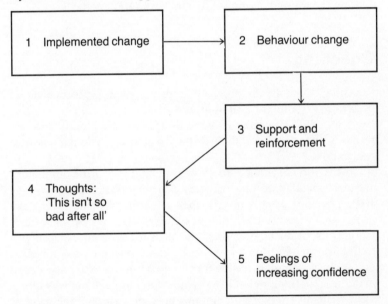

The key to success is the combination of force *and* support, the latter being conditional upon the occurrence of the changed behaviour. If support and encouragement are lacking then the strategy is unlikely to succeed since realigned thoughts (attitudes) and feelings will not result. The force and support strategy is really an extension of *behaviour modification* (see page 16).

When it comes to changing your own behaviour, as opposed to other people's, it is best to employ a slightly adapted version of behaviour modification. The steps are:

1 List the behaviours which you would like to change/improve.
2 Put the unwanted behaviours in order of importance.
3 Select one unwanted behaviour for change (ie an important one that you'd really like to improve).
4 Identify exactly when the unwanted behaviour occurs – the cues that trigger it.
5 Identify what pay-offs you get as a result of using the unwanted behaviour.
6 Be specific about the behaviour you want to change to.
7 See if you can do anything to change the cues so that the unwanted behaviour isn't triggered and the wanted behaviour is.
8 Work out how to reward yourself whenever you are successful in using the wanted, as opposed to the unwanted, behaviour.

Coaching

Coaching someone in order to improve their performance (ie behaviour) is a mixture of *appraisals* (see page 7) and *counselling* (see page 39). If appraisals were done more frequently and less formally than they usually are, they would be synonymous with coaching.

On-the-job coaching aims to help people to learn from experience in a low-key, routine way (see *Learning from experience* page 100). Coaching usually occurs when someone has made a mistake or not performed to the required standard. This is helpful because learning from mistakes cannot be taken for granted especially as frequently people don't even recognize a mistake as a mistake. However, coaching is just as fruitful after someone has succeeded in doing something well. Often people don't understand why things went well and are therefore not in a position to repeat the success. Coaching is the process that helps people to review, conclude and plan so that they make fewer mistakes and have more successes.

Collaborative

This is the name given to a style where 'I explain the situation and ask for ideas from the other person/people and together we agree what needs to be done'.

The collaborative style is a difficult one to adopt because if it is to be done genuinely it requires going into an interaction with an open mind about the eventual outcome. Many people find they are happier if they have a pre-prepared 'answer' or preferred solution. The essence of the collaborative approach is, however, to seek ideas from other people (see *Seeking ideas* on page 152) and, having sought them, actively to develop them there and then into an agreed solution. It is therefore a highly participative style.

Collaborating tends to be appropriate when:

- other people know at least as much, if not more, than you do (ie they are fully qualified to be equal partners in deciding on a course of action);
- the task is open-ended;
- there is time to reach consensus;
- the risks of getting it wrong first time round are not unacceptably high) ie there will be subsequent opportunities to review and refine);
- genuine commitment is essential to the success of the course of action.

Committees
See *Meetings* on pages 106–109

Common sense

Common sense is all those things that it is assumed just about everybody knows. Thus it is common sense to switch the lights off when you are the last to leave a room, and yet notices have to be stuck up to remind people. It is common sense to wear your seat belt when you drive your car, and yet the government had to introduce legislation to force people to do so. It is common sense to do all things in moderation and yet people still over-eat and drink too much.

People often say that the behavioural sciences are just common sense, and the 'just' is clearly meant to be dismissive. If people said 'behaving appropriately is common sense' that would be a compliment since the dictionary defines common sense as 'practical good sense and judgement'. It is the 'just' that turns it from a compliment to a snub.

The test of whether knowledge of behavioural matters is just common sense is to see whether possessing it succeeds in people doing things that would not otherwise occur to them. Let us check this out against the six basic *interpersonal skills* (see page 94). What might people possessing those skills do that would distinguish them from people without the skills? They would:

- be much faster at sizing up face-to-face situations by identifying the salient ingredients;
- set objectives that have a clear end result and are achievable within the context of the situation;
- select some key behaviours to use and some to avoid, that dovetail with the objectives;
- control their own behaviour so that it stays appropriate and matches the behaviours selected;
- succeed in influencing the other person's behaviour, via their own, so that it matches the behaviours required for the attainment of the objective;
- consciously monitor behaviour to check that it remains on course and make in-flight adjustments as necessary;
- more often than not, successfully achieve the objective.

In addition there are many smaller skills contained within the compass of the six big ones.

The plain fact is that most people do not do any of these things even though there is widespread acceptance that they make sense. Knowing it makes sense and doing it are two quite different things. Long live common sense, providing it includes doing and not just knowing.

Communication

Communication of one sort or another is absolutely vital so that people know what is expected of them and how they are doing. Unfortunately communication as a concept is so fundamental and so all-embracing that whilst it is popular to attribute every misunderstanding to 'poor communication' it doesn't get you very far.

Clearly good communication is entirely laudable but what in practice does it mean? That the receiver of a piece of information understands it exactly as the transmitter intended? That everyone knows everything they need to know? Or that, in addition, everyone knows everything it is nice to know?

Communication is a classic example of the need to be more specific and to break the behaviours involved down into categories (see *Categories of behaviour* on page 26). This is not to deny its importance, merely to bemoan the fact that communication is meaningless until some behaviours are pinpointed.

Complacency

Complacency is a friend of the *status quo* and an enemy of improvement. Complacent people see no need to learn and are content to replicate their current performance (ie behaviour). This is an especially tempting frame of mind when things are apparently successful. The problem is that nothing ever stands still for long and sooner or later the complacent performer is overtaken by events. When change exceeds the rate of learning that spells trouble (see *Resistance to change* on page 145). When, on the other hand, learning exceeds the rate of change we keep at least one step ahead. Continuous improvement involves learning from successes just as much as learning from failures. For more on the process of doing this see *Learning from experience* on page 100 and *Self development* on page 154.

Compromise
See *Win-win* on pages 174–175

Conflict

Conflicts between people are inevitable. Whenever you have a difference of opinion with someone that is a conflict. There are conflicts with a small 'c' and conflicts with a big 'C' but they are all conflicts.

Broadly there are three different ways of reacting to conflict:

1 *Avoiding the conflict*
Typically this involves:
denying it exists
circumventing the person/people with whom you are in conflict
deciding not to make it explicit or to raise it.

2 *Diffusing the conflict*
This involves:
smoothing things over, 'pouring oil on troubled waters'
saying you'll come back to it (as opposed to dealing with it there and then)
only dealing with minor points, not the major issues.

3 *Facing the conflict*
This involves:
openly admitting it exists
explicitly raising it as an issue.

All three approaches are genuine options when conflicts arise. There may be occasions when it is best to let it go (why win the battle but lose the war?) and there will be other occasions when some pussy-footing is appropriate. In theory, however, facing conflict rather than avoiding it or diffusing it offers the most potential. But *how* you face it makes all the difference. You can face it aggressively or assertively.

Facing conflict aggressively means:

- being secretive about your real objective
- exaggerating your case
- refusing to concede that the other person has a valid point
- belittling the other person's points
- repeating your case dogmatically
- disagreeing
- interrupting the other person.

Facing conflict assertively means:
- being open about your objective
- establishing what the other person's objective is
- searching for common ground
- stating your case clearly
- understanding the other person's case

- producing ideas to solve the differences
- developing the other person's ideas
- summarizing to check understanding/agreement.

For more on assertive, as opposed to aggressive, behaviour, see *Assertiveness* on page 8.

Conscious behaviour

Being conscious of your behaviour is considered by most people to be the opposite of behaving naturally. Conscious behaviour is relatively unpopular because people object:

- that it takes effort and deliberate concentration
- that it impairs overall performance because concentrating on one aspect of behaviour means other aspects go unchecked
- that it is unethical because the behaviour is being artificially created rather than occurring naturally.

Despite these objections making behaviour conscious and deliberate is an inevitable, but thankfully temporary, stage during the acquisition of new or additional behaviours (see *Skilful behaviour*, page 155). All so-called natural behaviour, with the obvious exception of some basic reflexes, was at some stage unnatural in the sense that you couldn't do it effortlessly or skilfully. The advantages of conscious behaviour are:

- that it makes you more aware of your behaviour and the effect it is having on other people
- that it forces you to employ behaviours that you would not otherwise use.

Rejecting the need for conscious behaviour is a recipe for standing still and not expanding your repertoire of behaviours. Some rather brash advice is, 'If at first you can't make it, fake it'.

Consultative

The name given to a style where 'I explain the situation and ask for ideas from the other person/people and then I decide what needs to be done'.

The consultative style is far easier to adopt than the *collaborative* style (see page 32) because at the end of the day responsibility for taking the decision resides with the user of the style. The main problem with the consultative style is that people often mistake it for the collaborative style and incorrectly assume that they will also be involved in fashioning the final decision. This is an unhelpful expectation which, once built up, can lead to considerable resentment when it becomes clear that what they have been asked for is consultation not collaboration. The answer is to make it clear from the outset which style is being used and why.

Consulting tends to be appropriate when:

- you don't have a monopoly on the information and experience; other people involved have relevant knowledge and experience
- the task is open-ended
- a decision must be taken but not immediately or urgently
- the risks of a mistake are unacceptably high (ie after consulting people you are going to make the final decision)
- the numbers of people are not so vast that it is impossible to contemplate consulting them
- genuine commitment is highly desirable – but not absolutely vital.

Content

Whenever you say something there are two aspects: the content of whatever you say and the way you say it or, in other words, the behaviour. To understand truly the meaning of what someone says to you, you need to take both aspects into account. If, for example, someone said 'It is 12 o'clock' the content conveys an unremarkable piece of factual information that is either correct or false. However, the behaviour of the speaker could convey a variety of different messages without any alteration to the content. They could say it in:

- a matter of fact manner
- an exasperated manner
- a defeatist manner
- an accusing manner
- a questioning manner

and so on.

If you only attend to the content message you will often misunderstand what the speaker is trying to convey – likewise, if you only attend to the behaviour message. Both aspects need to be heeded in parallel in the hazardous business of transmitting and receiving verbal communications.

Counselling

Counselling is where one person, the counsellor, helps another person, the counsellee, to solve a personal problem of some kind. The counsellor may be a superior helping a subordinate whose performance is being impaired by the effects of a personal problem, or a colleague helping a peer, or a professional counsellor, such as a marriage guidance counsellor, helping a client. Potentially *anyone* can counsel anyone else but, as we shall see, counselling is a process that calls for some special behavioural skills on the part of the counsellor.

Personal problems come in all sorts of shapes and sizes. They are hard to pinpoint very precisely because so much depends on the eye of the beholder. A problem that overwhelms one person is merely a minor irritation, or even accepted as an interesting challenge, to another. Probably the easiest way to think of a problem is to view it as a gap. The gap is the difference between the current situation and the desired one. So if a person is in debt or unhappy in their marriage or with some aspect of their work, they have a problem. Sometimes problems are more felt, or imagined, than real. If, for example, someone felt they were being exploited, then they would have a problem even though they might be imagining it.

If you are to help people solve their personal problems, there is something about problems of this kind it is vital to appreciate: the counsellee always owns the problem. The idea that someone *owns* their problems in the same way that they might own clothes or a pair of shoes might seem strange, but it is a key concept in counselling. This is because:

- it makes it *less* likely that the counsellor will take over the counsellee's problem
- and *more* likely that the counsellor will help the counsellee to accept responsibility both for the problem and for doing something about it.

Quite understandably, many counsellors, especially if they have do-gooder tendencies, are prone to interfering too much and imposing a solution, *their* solution, on the counsellee. The temptation to do this is made even stronger by counsellees who are only too willing to 'delegate' responsibility for solving the problem. Personal problems by their very nature cannot be delegated. They belong to, and have to be solved by, the counsellee. It is this simple fact that makes counselling a more skilful business than might be supposed.

Effective counselling is no mean feat and there are some behaviours that are crucial to the process. Here is a checklist of all the main ingredients!

Before counselling

Set up the interview by:

- spotting the need by noticing unexplained changes in people's behaviour and work performance
- listen to the grapevine to see if it alerts you to the existence of any troublesome personal problems
- organize an uninterrupted period of time, 30 minutes minimum, 60 minutes maximum.

When counselling

Encourage people to talk by:

- offering reassurance

- asking open-ended questions
- sitting at a 90 degrees angle to them
- showing they have your undivided attention
- opening with a non-threatening enquiry
- listening hard
- playing-back what you've heard
- encouraging them to say more.

Help people to think their problems through by:

- admitting your own fallibility
- offering relevant information but banning all opinions or criticisms
- asking questions to solicit ideas
- suggesting some tentative ideas in the form of questions ('How about . . . ?').

Let people find their own solution by:

- supporting their solution
- agreeing an action plan and review date
- leaving the door open for their return.

After counselling

- carry on as if it had never happened
- keep confidences to yourself
- continue watching for signs of personal problems that are affecting people's performances.

Creative thinking

This is a way of thinking and, more importantly, a way of behaving which succeeds in relating, or linking, things or ideas which were previously unrelated.

Creative thinking (or lateral thinking as it is sometimes called) is most helpful when tackling open-end problems where you can:

- challenge the constraints because they aren't fixed
- envisage many alternative, equally viable solutions.

In denary mathematics there is no point in applying creative thinking to the problem $1 + 1 =$ because there is one correct answer. On the other hand, the problem 'In how many ways can you interpret $1 + 1 = ?$' has dozens of possible answers which creative thinking would help to generate. Most interesting and major problems in life are open-ended even though people often treat them as though they were closed-ended.

Creative thinking doesn't solve problems, not even open-ended ones; it merely gives more and better alternatives to choose between. Creative thinking is therefore not an alternative to analytical (or vertical) thinking. To solve open-ended problems successfully you need both sorts of thinking: creative thinking to generate lots of ideas and analytical thinking to tidy up afterwards by evaluating the worthwhileness of the ideas and deciding which to implement.

There are lots of techniques to aid creative thinking mainly because people, left to their own devices, are so bad at it. The argument is that to happen at all creative thinking needs to be special. Each technique provides a temporary haven, or protection, from the habits of analytical thinking.

Here are four of the better known creative thinking techniques.

Challenging assumptions

Simply write down the initial definition of a problem and underline *all* the words in it that are debatable or challengeable. Then take each underlined word in turn and question it.

Attribute listing

List all the attributes or characteristics of the thing involved in a problem. Then take each attribute in turn and use it as a trigger to spark off ideas.

Random stimulation

When you aren't making progress with a problem or when you want some novel inputs, use a dictionary to provide a random word. Simply think of a number in advance (or throw some dice, or use a table of random numbers) and turn up that page in a dictionary. Use a second random number to select a word on the page. Then spend three to five minutes generating ideas that come when the problem and the random word are thought about in combination. Often the random word is used to generate further words which themselves link up to the problem. In some cases a pun on the word may be used, or its opposite, or the word spelled slightly differently. There is no one correct way to use it. The word is used in order to get things going – not to prove or solve anything.

Brainstorming

A formal opportunity for people to make suggestions they would not otherwise dare make for fear of being thought stupid or being laughed at. In summary brainstorming involves the following stages:

1 The chairman states the problem.
2 The group join in restating the problem listing statements in the form 'How to . . . ?'
3 The group selects a basic restatement and the chairman writes down 'In how many ways can we . . . ?'
4 The chairman explains and displays brainstorming rules:
   Think wild
   Cross-fertilize
   Suspend judgement
   Go for quantity.
5 The group do a warm-up session on a neutral problem – 'Other uses for a . . . ?'
6 The group brainstorm:
   Aim for 100 ideas in 20 minutes
   Display ideas on flipcharts
   Number each idea
   Include 30-second silences to aid cross-fertilization.
7 The chairman selects the wildest idea 'Let's see if we can make something of . . .'

You may be worried that the very formality of these structured techniques will inhibit, rather than encourage, creative thinking. This particularly applies if you regard creative thinking as essentially a spontaneous happening. The trouble with this is that you would have to wait until people were in the right mood to be creative. The idea of the techniques is to use them to engineer the conditions that trigger creative thinking. Make the right environment and creative behaviour will flourish.

Criticism

Criticism is a behaviour that people either over-indulge in or shy away from. Those who over-indulge tend to believe that people respond best to a punitive regime that keeps them on their toes. Those who avoid criticism favour harmonious relationships and a high popularity rating and fear that anything resembling criticism would cause upsets and spoil the pleasant atmosphere.

People have a right to know how they are doing and what they can do to improve. If there are aspects of their performance which are unsatisfactory then feedback is essential so that they are helped to see the error of their ways and how to make corrections. Feedback therefore oscillates between containing good news (see *Praise* on page 135) and bad news. Where the feedback contains bad news it is likely to be seen as criticism and provoke a defensive reaction.

How is it possible to criticize people constructively so as to improve their performance rather than lead to a slanging match? The following table contrasts effective and less effective forms of criticism:

Ineffective criticism	*Effective criticism*
1 Criticism that involves use of the personal 'you', eg 'You're making too many mistakes on the word processor, Sue.' Criticism like this is aimed more at the person ('you') than at the person's behaviour. Accusations are almost always taken as a 'discount' by the person, which erodes their self confidence and exacerbates the problem.	1 Criticism using a situational description, eg 'Sue, I notice an increase in mistakes on the word processor.' This is a more dispassionate statement that doesn't point an accusing finger at the person. Instead it focuses straightforwardly on the problem.

2 Sweeping criticism that offers no analysis of the situation. This sort of criticism is too generalized to be helpful and leaves the person smarting from the criticism but with no notion of what they can do to effect an improvement.

2 An analysis of the problem that pinpoints cause and effect.

3 Criticism that contains no constructive suggestions on what could be done to improve.

3 Criticism in order to be constructive needs to generate ideas on what could be done to improve the situation with eventual agreement on a course of action.

4 Criticism done as a monologue with one person doing all the talking.

4 Criticism done participatively where both people join together to analyse the situation, generate ideas and arrive at an agreed solution.

5 Criticism that skirts around the issue with half truths and innuendos.

5 Criticism that is honest, straightforward and candid.

6 Criticism done in public with other people present. This is not only regarded as humiliating for the person being criticized but it also has an adverse effect on the bystanders who tend to take sides.

6 Individual criticism given in private is usually more acceptable and more appropriate.

Customer satisfaction

Customer satisfaction is just as dependent on behavioural factors (in fact often more so) as on the quality of the product itself.

Customer satisfaction, unlike behaviour, is an internal feeling which cannot be directly observed. Putting it at its simplest, a customer feels satisfied when the product and the behaviour they receive meets their needs and exceeds their expectations. Diagrammatically it looks like this:

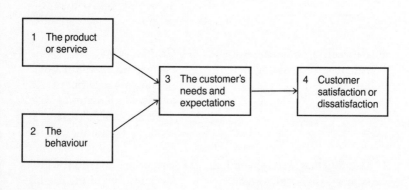

Since satisfaction is a subjective feeling the customer always decides what is good or bad service on his or her own terms. You may *know* your product is best and be able to prove it objectively but the customer's subjective feelings are always the ultimate adjudicator.

Let us look briefly at each of the ingredients in the above diagram.

1 The product or service

The quality of the product or service is obviously a factor in influencing customer satisfaction or dissatisfaction. However, some people make the mistake of thinking that it is the sole factor and put a disproportionate amount of energy into perfecting the product. This is fine providing the product still meets the customer's needs. If it does not then the finer points will not be appreciated by the customer and not, therefore, result in a feeling of satisfaction.

2 The behaviour

The quality of the behaviour of everyone in the organization who has any dealings, however 'trivial', with the customer is another major factor in influencing customer satisfaction or dissatisfaction. The behaviour of, say, a skilful salesperson can be an even more important factor than the quality of the product.

3 The customer's needs and expectations

There are two factors here of equal importance in the equation. The customer's needs are what he or she wants the product or service to do for them. However, even if a product or service meets these needs, unfortunately this is unlikely to result in customer satisfaction. It merely results in a customer who is neither satisfied nor dissatisfied. This is because the customer *expects* the product to meet his needs. When it doesn't, the customer feels dissatisfied, but when it does, the customer does not necessarily feel satisfied; they merely got what they expected and that in itself is not remarkable to the customer. (Remember, the customer always decides on their own terms.)

So, meeting people's needs is not sufficient to guarantee customer satisfaction. There has to be something extra that *exceeds* the customer's expectations. The easiest way to score these extra 'brownie points' and delight the customer is behavioural rather than anything to do with the product, which is most clearly seen in cases where something has gone wrong. If you take an airline example where, let us suppose, the flight has been delayed or luggage has been lost (ie where the quality of the product is flawed), the behaviour of the airline staff can more than offset temporary lapses in the quality of the product. This is because in this situation the customers have a problem, albeit not of their own creation, and tend to be grateful for any help that is offered to solve 'their' problem. The existence of the problem has effectively lowered their expectations and customers with low expectations are much easier to satisfy than customers with high ones.

4 *Customer satisfaction or dissatisfaction*

We have already established that customer satisfaction is a subjective feeling rather than anything more tangible or objective. The other important point to appreciate is that customer satisfaction is not the direct opposite of dissatisfaction. There are two separate scales as follows:

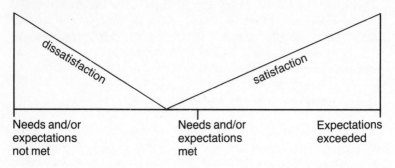

Needs and/or	Needs and/or	Expectations
expectations	expectations	exceeded
not met	met	

Products and/or behaviours which fail to meet customers' needs or to match up to expectations obviously will create a state of dissatisfaction. When this occurs the customer is likely to complain and to take his business elsewhere.

Products and/or behaviours which meet customers' needs and match expectations create a sort of mental state where the customer is neither satisfied nor dissatisfied. When this occurs the customer is likely to experiment with different products and not to develop any 'brand loyalty'.

Only where the product and/or behaviours meet the customers' needs *and exceed* their expectations are customers likely to feel positively satisfied. When this occurs customers are likely to express their delight, sometimes directly to the supplier and certainly to colleagues and contacts. 'Word of mouth' is the most effective marketing in existence.

Since behaviour is always overt it has a direct impact on the customer's reactions. Behaviour breeds behaviour. The way people behave in their dealings with the customer is often *the* deciding factor in putting the customer positively on the 'satisfaction scale'. The interesting thing is that there is nothing especially difficult or clever about the behaviours that create a satisfied customer. Indeed the behaviours that help rather than hinder are often quite small and easy to dismiss as trivial. This confirms the old adage 'it's the little things that count'. For a list of the *helpful behaviours* that make all the difference see page 84.

Delegation

Delegating is an extraordinarily difficult thing to do effectively despite its apparent desirability. People get into a muddle about what to delegate and having done so how to monitor and retain some control over the delegatee.

What to delegate is simple. You delegate responsibilities (ie tasks) which belong to you together with the appropriate authority (ie powers) to carry out those responsibilities. To delegate responsibilities without authority is not real delegation since the delegatee has to keep running to you for permission to do anything. It is impossible to delegate accountability. That is retained by the delegator (ie the buck always stops with the delegator).

Since delegation is not abdication, precisely because the delegator retains accountability, it is vital to safeguard your interests by monitoring at appropriate intervals. What is appropriate will depend on the experience and trustworthiness of the delegatee. It is best to agree how you will monitor and with what frequency as a vital part of the delegation routine.

Delegating tends to be appropriate when:

- other people can be trusted to perform well
- the task is within the capabilities of the people it is delegated to and can be done better and at less expense by them
- the task is appropriate, ie it does *not* involve overall policy making or the selection, training or appraisal of the manager's immediate subordinates
- giving people opportunities to learn and develop from experience.

Depression

Depression is an unwanted feeling that frequently spills over into behaviour. Fortunately depression is a preventable feeling but it is vital to read the section on *Preventing unwanted feelings* (on page 138) before reading the remainder of this section because what follows assumes you have understood the two options involved.

Unproductive feelings of depression hinder your behaviour in a variety of ways. All or some of the following might apply to you:

- You withdraw into a shell.
- You lose zest/enthusiasm for anything. Nothing seems worthwhile.
- You lose your sense of humour.
- You are listless and can't settle to any activity.
- You become selfish and overdemanding. It's all take and no give.
- You cry/weep and become pessimistic, running the risk of alienating people around you.
- You have difficulty getting up in the morning and facing a new day.
- You eat/drink too much.

Your feelings of depression are always triggered by some external event or happening. Typical examples might be when:

- you are reminded nostalgically of a day/event you enjoyed in the past
- someone close to you dies
- you realize you are getting old
- you are alone with no-one to talk to
- a thoroughly enjoyable activity or friendship comes to an end
- you see a photograph or possession of someone you miss
- you are away from your home and family
- you identify with someone who is upset or with a tear-jerking play/book or piece of music
- you are in pain or after you have been ill/had an operation
- you suffer a serious set-back (ie being declared redundant, being unemployed, failing at something you very much wanted to succeed at)
- the weather is grey and dull.

Clearly, ideas for changing the events that trigger your depression will depend on the exact circumstances, but here are some thought-starters that might help you to arrive at a feasible plan:

- Keep a depression log and identify when you feel depressed, for how long and in what circumstances, then plan to avoid situations that depress you.
- Keep a happiness log and identify what makes you happy. Plan to increase your exposure to situations that trigger happiness.
- Steer clear of depressed/sad people.
- Don't spend time alone. Go and see someone.
- Keep fit.
- Keep active.
- Go for a holiday in February (or whatever time of year tends to trigger your depression).
- Resist the temptation to go back and visit places where you were once happy. Avoid trips down memory lane.
- Concentrate on tackling small tasks with a tangible output that can be accomplished in one go (frequent mini successes are better than infrequent big ones).
- Leap out of bed as soon as you wake up and say out loud 'Today is the first day of the rest of my life'.
- Whenever you see yourself in a mirror give yourself a smile and a wink.

Rather than modify anything to do with the external events that trigger your depression you might decide to go for option 2 and identify the thoughts or beliefs that herald your depression and examine them for possible replacements. Typical thoughts for feelings of depression are:

- I was happy then. I am not happy now and never will be again.
- There is no point.
- Oh, how I miss . . .
- I wish I was younger/back home/with him or her again.
- If only I could have my time again.
- This is terrible, anybody would get depressed in these circumstances.

And, finally, here are some thought-starters on ways of replacing unrealistic thoughts and beliefs that provoke feelings of depression so that they become more realistic and less likely to hinder your behaviour:

- Nothing whatsoever can *make* me sad. I choose whether to be depressed or not.
- I owe it to myself and everyone else to . . .
- What is past is past. It's *now* that counts.
- Why should I feel depressed about that?
- Nothing is *terrible* but some things that happen are unfortunate.
- What am I trying to avoid by feeling depressed?

Difficulty stating

Difficulty stating is a behaviour where you point out the difficulties, snags and problems with something someone else has said.

Classic examples are: 'The snag with that would be . . .' 'We wouldn't be able to do that because . . .' 'The problem with that is . . .' This category is used to cover difficulty stating in relation to the content of what others have said as well as difficulty stating about the context of the interaction. So remarks like 'This is an absolute shambles. We aren't getting anywhere'; 'We are running out of time again'; 'I can't understand a word you are saying', are all included in this difficulty stating category. Difficulty stating contributions do not actually contain a disagreement. If a contribution does contain both disagreement and a difficulty state, it is classified as *disagreeing* (see page 54).

Difficulty stating is a fairly widespread behaviour. It happens more than twice as often as disagreeing. In a typical interaction difficulty stating accounts for 11 per cent of all the spoken behaviours. The reason why difficulty stating is more popular than out and out disagreeing is presumably because it isn't as courageous or foolhardy. When you explicitly disagree you leave people in no doubt about where you stand. Difficulty stating is by contrast a 'softer' option with less risk of upsetting people.

Difficulty stating often paves the way for ideas to be developed (see *Building* page 25). 'Playing devil's advocate' acts as a stimulus for people to work hard in either explaining the merits of their idea or to improve it in the wake of stated difficulties. The irony is that whenever you indulge in difficulty stating you are half way to developing an idea. The sequence of events most people seem to go through is:

1 Listen to somebody else's idea.
2 Analyse the idea and find fault with it.

If you speak out at this point in the sequence then you are difficulty stating. However, if you don't speak and press on as follows:

3 Think of a way of improving the idea to overcome the fault you have detected.
4 Suggest your improvement. If you speak at this point, you are building.

As we have seen, pointing out difficulties is a very common behaviour but is one of the riskier ones because research shows that it is far from certain how people will take it. Marginally, the most likely reaction is to offer some clarification or explanation. However, many people take umbrage and start disagreeing or, if you persist with difficulties, may give up and go and find someone more positive to talk to. You need to watch carefully to see whether pointing out difficulties is hindering or helping the proceedings.

Directive

This is the name given to a style where 'I decide what needs to be done and I tell the person/people what to do and how to do it'.

This is a style that most people find relatively easy to adopt, certainly easier than the alternatives of being *Consultative* (see page 38), *Collaborative* (see page 32) or *Delegating* (see page 49).

Directing tends to be appropriate when:

- you are better informed and more experienced than others who are involved (ie you literally do know best)
- the task is close-ended
- a decision must be taken immediately
- the risks of a mistake are unacceptably high
- large numbers of people are involved
- genuine commitment is not vital.

Disagreeing

Disagreeing is a behaviour where you *explicitly* disagree with something someone else has said. Implicit disagreements are categorized as *difficulty stating* (see page 52).

You can voice your disagreement in one of two ways. There are flat disagreements, such as 'No' or 'I disagree', or there are disagreements accompanied with some reasons or explanation such as 'I disagree with that because . . .'. Interestingly, in emotionally charged situations unreasoned flat disagreements tend to predominate. This happens in domestic rows and often in management/ union confrontations. The flat disagreements occur as protagonists project their entrenched positions.

Disagreements with reasons are much easier to handle because, of course, the reasons are the key to overcoming the disagreement and moving on. However, there is a hazard. When you disagree with reasons it is highly likely that the person you are disagreeing with will interrupt you before you have finished explaining your reasons. This is particularly so if you have a number of reasons to proffer. It is as though the explicit announcement that you are in disagreement attracts all their attention and detracts from their preparedness to hear you out. The answer is to reverse the order of events; give your reasons first (best to ration them so that you advance one reason at a time rather than blowing the whole lot in one speech) and then finish by saying something like '. . . and that is why I disagree'. This has the advantage of getting attention focused on the reasons for the disagreement rather than on the fact of the disagreement. When disagreeing is done this way, interruptions are less likely and, even more important, disagreements are dealt with more constructively.

In the average problem-solving conversation disagreeing absorbs six per cent of all the behaviours. People tend to overestimate the amount of explicit disagreeing that has occurred and to expect it to be on a par with *building* (see page 25). In fact disagreeing, even at six per cent tends to be double the amount of building.

After a disagreement has occurred people either respond by attempting to clarify (the assumption being that a misunderstanding is at the root of the disagreement) or by disagreeing back. It is interesting how often people get locked into a disagreeing 'spiral' where one disagreement breeds another which, in turn, breeds another and so on.

When someone persistently disagrees with you the most effective antidote is to resist the temptation to go on the defensive or offensive and to ask them for an idea (see *Seeking ideas* on page 152). They will more likely be provoked into being more constructive and it gives you the right to respond.

Discounts

Discounts are the reverse of *strokes* (see page 156). Discounts are behaviours that diminish people. Some examples are:

- ignoring other people's ideas
- keeping people waiting
- not consulting or involving people in decisions which affect them
- asking for suggestions when you're already clear on your decision
- hurrying up rather than listening
- closing an issue before everyone feels heard
- over-explaining obvious things as if the listener were incapable of grasping the problem himself
- being condescending
- refusing to acknowledge someone's expressed feelings
- using jargon
- name dropping
- criticizing the person (as opposed to something the person has done).

Discounts help people to feel inadequate, they erode self-confidence and lead to resentment and over-cautious behaviour. In short, discounts tell people they are 'not OK'. When people discount *themselves* ('I don't know much about this but. . . . I've probably got this all wrong but. . . . I'm sure to make a mess of this. . . .') they have probably been over-exposed to discounting, no longer feel confident and have therefore stopped being clear, direct and open.

The way to stop discounting other people is to use your Adult (see *Ego-states* on page 57) to face the problem squarely instead of indulging in niggling discounts. This raises the intriguing question of how to criticize someone's performance in a constructive way that leads to improved performance rather than reduced self-confidence. The contrast between effective criticism and ineffective criticism is drawn in the section on *Criticism* (on page 44).

The other issue is how to stop discounting yourself in relation to other people. Self-discounting stems from an *'I'm not OK'* posture (see page 123). Examples are:

- 'I don't have good ideas compared to the rest of the people here.'
- 'They aren't interested in what I have to say.'
- 'I wish I could express myself better.'
- 'If I don't try, I can't fail.'
- 'The best way to keep out of trouble is to keep my mouth shut and never volunteer for anything.'

The way to break this vicious circle is to use your Adult to check reality and to force yourself (initially) to go at risk and try things in situations where the probability of success is high. When people give you strokes accept them by saying to yourself 'I deserved that. I am OK'. Gradually self-confidence develops and, even though many of the old 'I'm not OK' feelings remain, your behaviour is no longer at their mercy.

Ego-states

Ego-states are the core concept in *transactional analysis* (TA) (see page 167). An important and recurring assumption in TA is that we have learned to behave in certain ways. There are three main modes of behaviour used by everyone, though their predominance varies from individual to individual. These ways of behaving are called ego-states and their development started in early childhood. According to TA theory, experiences are 'recorded' in the brain and stored there as if on video tape. Experiences from childhood – what was learnt from and taught by parents or equivalents, perceptions of events and the feelings associated with those events – are captured on the tapes and provide the sources for *current* behaviour. As we shall see, in TA it is assumed that the early learning on the tapes cannot be erased, even if it is no longer appropriate, but it can be updated as we learn from experience.

The three ego-states are called Parent, Adult and Child. In TA they are distinguished from *real* parents, adults and children by giving each a capital letter.

Parent

Parent behaviour stems from feelings about what is proper, right and wrong. This provides discipline and protection. The Parent tends to speak in a dogmatic way with a heavy emphasis on controlling. Parent behaviour is subdivided into:

Critical Parent
CP behaviour is critical, prejudicial, moralizing or punitive. Typical non-verbal clues are a pointed index finger, shaking head, hand-wringing, arms folded, foot tapping, wrinkled brow, sighing, impatient snorts and grunts. Typical verbal clues are 'always, never, remember, you ought to know better, you should do better, don't do that, you should never do that, that's wrong, stupid, ridiculous, absurd, how dare you'.

Nurturing Parent
NP behaviour is nurturing, protective, sympathetic and comforting. Non-verbal examples are: a comforting touch, patting a person on the shoulder, consoling sounds. Verbal examples are: 'there, there, you poor thing, try again, don't worry'.

Adult

Adult behaviour involves gathering information, evaluating it and using it to make, and implement decisions. The Adult has the capacity to monitor and, if necessary, update Parent and Child tapes. Adult behaviour stems from thinking rather than feeling. Non-verbal examples are: postures indicating interest, listening, thinking and generally being 'with it'. Verbal examples are: 'why, what, where, when, who, how, alternatives, possible, probably, relatively, practical, feasible'.

Child

Child behaviour stems from feelings, either of joy or of sorrow, and therefore tends to be spontaneous. Child behaviour is subdivided into:

Natural Child

NC behaviour is entirely dictated by feelings; it includes being impulsive, inquisitive, curious, affectionate and playful. NC is also fearful, self-indulgent, self-centred, rebellious and aggressive. Non-verbal examples are: tears, temper tantrums, no answer, biting lower lip, downcast eyes, shoulder shrugging. Verbal examples are: 'Look at me!, Nobody loves me. That's mine, can't, won't, that's fun, I love you, whoopee!'

Adapted Child

AC behaviour is a toned-down version of Natural Child: it is literally an adaptation of completely natural impulses so that they are more acceptable to other people. Non-verbal examples are: giggling, teasing, flirting, pouting and whining. Verbal examples are: 'please, thank you, I wish, I'll try, please help me, I don't care, I don't know'.

These three basic ways of behaving can be used as a shorthand for analysing transactions between people. This is usually done dia-grammatically by plotting the stimulus and response behaviours between speakers. A transaction is a unit of interaction between people consisting of a communication from A to B and the resulting response from B to A.

Transactions between people can be complementary or crossed. A transaction between two people is complementary when a message sent by one ego-state gets the expected response from the other person. Here are some examples:

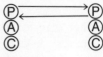

'Unions are far too powerful nowadays.'

'They certainly are. They are ruining the economy!'

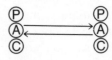

'What time is the meeting today?'

'This afternoon at two thirty.'

This may seem laborious but with practice the Adult can cope. A skilful Adult can monitor by exception, only going on 'red alert' when something unexpected happens.

As we have seen, an important practical implication of TA is that you can use your behaviour to elicit the reactions you want from other people. This happens whether we consciously harness the process or not. Here are some examples of how to hook different ego-states in others.

- Acknowledge their current ego-state (vital, or else they'll feel discounted) and then invite them to move to Adult by:
      asking a question
      stating some facts
      asking for options/their preference
- Invite them to move to Nurturing Parent by:
      asking for help
      asking for advice
      communicating your fears/worries
- Invite them to move to Natural Child by:
      being one yourself
      showing the funny side of the situation
      going to Nurturing Parent
      being enthusiastic
      showing an unconventional/novel way of looking at things.

For other concepts from transactional analysis see *Strokes*, page 156), *Discounts*, page 55, *Games*, page 71, *OKness*, page 123.

Emotion
See *Feelings* on pages 66–69

Empathy
See *Rapport* on pages 144–145

Face-to-face situations

A face-to-face situation is any situation where you physically meet with one person or more. It might be an informal discussion with someone you bumped into along the corridor or a formal committee meeting with an agenda, minute-taking and all the other paraphernalia.

Face-to-face situations are important occasions because all aspects of your behaviour are simultaneously on display; what you look like and what you say together with all the non-verbal accompaniments. By contrast, *telephone behaviour* (see page 164) is much reduced since in that situation people can only hear what you say and how you say it.

There are six key questions to ask of any situation you encounter:

1 Is the task/problem/subject matter to be discussed complex or routine?
2 On balance, who has the most know-how, you or the other people involved in the face-to-face discussion?
3 Is time very tight (as in a crisis) or is there sufficient time to discuss all aspects thoroughly before reaching a decision?
4 Is commitment from everyone essential or merely highly desirable?
5 Are the risks of making a mistake unacceptably high (financially and/or physically and/or from a credibility point of view) or are the risks within acceptable limits?
6 How many people will be present at the face-to-face discussion, just one other person, or a small group of say 6–8 or a medium sized group of 9–15, or a large group of 15 plus?

Clearly some face-to-face situations are more important than others. Your behaviour becomes increasingly crucial to success in direct proportion to the number of the following factors that are characteristic of the situation:

• You are consciously aware of wanting to achieve something/an objective.
• You judge that your characteristic mode of behaviour isn't going to be appropriate.
• You have a key role to play in the interaction, ie you are going to be in the 'chair'.
• You want to *influence* the other person(s) in order to achieve your objective.
• You want to *impress* the other person(s).
• The situation is *delicate*, ie people are likely to be touchy/emotional.

- The people involved have *conflicting* objectives.
- You are likely to feel out of your depth or lacking in confidence.
- You want to *help* the other person(s) to achieve their objective.

Feedback

Feedback is an essential part of learning. Maybe it is an overstatement but it is almost true to say no feedback, no learning. Certainly in the absence of feedback people find it impossible to sustain good performance. A dramatic illustration of this is to take a dart player who, say seven times out of ten, can hit the triple twenty. If you deprive him of the usual feedback which is normal to a dart thrower by, for example, using a tray to prevent him seeing where the dart hit the board, you can see his performance decline even though you haven't interfered with his normal stance, aim or throwing of the darts.

Most people are starved of feedback even though they have a basic right to know how they are doing and what they can do to improve. People lack feedback for a variety of reasons:

- a reluctance to solicit feedback in case in doing so they hear something they'd rather not, such as criticism
- a reluctance to proffer feedback in case it is seen as condescending or upsetting the person
- a lack of skill in receiving feedback in an open-minded, non-defensive way, that leads to learning
- a lack of skill in giving feedback in a helpful, constructive non-judgemental way that leads to a specific action plan for improvement.

Of course feedback can be good as well as bad. Since most people spend most of their time doing more things right than they do wrong it is surprising that there isn't more positive feedback. Most people work in an environment where if you get it right no one says anything ('You're paid to get it right. You want praise as well?') but if you get it wrong all hell breaks out. Unfortunately punitive rather than positive feedback is only a fraction of the story and leads to all sorts of unhelpful behaviours on the part of people who suffer under a punitive regime (see *Punishment* on page 142 and *Positive reinforcement* on page 134).

The essential skills of giving and receiving feedback are listed under *Appraisals* on page 7 and *Counselling* on page 39.

Feeling hurt

Hurt is an unwanted feeling that frequently spills over into behaviour. Fortunately hurt is a preventable feeling but it is vital to read the section on *Preventing unwanted feelings* (on page 138) before reading the remainder of this section because what follows assumes you have understood the two options involved.

Unproductive feelings of hurt hinder your behaviour in a variety of ways. All or some of the following might apply to you:

- You fall silent/stop contributing/pull your horns in.
- You snap back to even the score.
- You plot your revenge/plan how to get your own back.
- You withdraw to lick your wounds in private.
- You sulk/cry.

Your hurt is always triggered by some external event or happening. Typical examples might be when:

- someone you hold in high esteem criticizes your behaviour or your appearance
- someone puts you down in front of others
- you have been on a self-congratulatory 'high' and someone deflates you with a sarcastic/snide/critical remark
- someone cuts you dead or forgets your name and/or that they have met you before
- someone ignores you/is oblivious to your sensitive feelings
- you learn that someone has been gossiping about you behind your back
- you discover you have been passed over/left out (eg from being invited to a party).
- someone makes an innocent remark that you interpret as critical of you (if the cap fits wear it!).

Clearly, ideas for changing the events that trigger your feelings of hurt will depend on the exact circumstances, but here are some thought-starters that might help you to arrive at a feasible plan:

- Keep a hurt diary and plan to avoid people or situations where you are vulnerable.
- When someone criticizes you, respond immediately by asking them a question: 'Why do you think that?' 'What do you suggest I do about it?' 'When do you notice me doing that?'
- When you meet someone you haven't met for some time, immediately give your name and remind them where they previously met you. This way you'll never know whether they had forgotten you or not and therefore can't be offended.
- When going into a situation where you feel vulnerable or unsure of yourself take a supporter with you.

Rather than modify anything to do with the external events that trigger your hurt you might decide to go for option 2 and identify the thoughts or beliefs that herald your feelings of hurt and examine them for possible replacements. Typical thoughts for feelings of hurt are:

- They are criticizing me. I knew I wasn't good enough for them.
- Ouch! That hurts!
- That is below the belt – it isn't fair.
- They are right. I am worthless. Foolish of me to imagine otherwise.
- They shouldn't hurt my feelings.
- What will everyone think of me?
- My secret is out. I'm done for. No-one will like me any more.

And, finally, here are some thought-starters on ways of replacing unrealistic thoughts and beliefs that provoke feelings of hurt so that they become more realistic and less likely to hinder your behaviour:

- They are criticizing me. How interesting. I stand to learn/gain from this.
- No-one can hurt me. I decide whether to feel hurt or not.
- They aren't criticizing me – merely my actions or my appearance and I can easily change those if I want to.
- I don't need their approval. I'd like it, but I don't *need* it.

- I can't please everybody. At least 50 per cent of the people I meet won't like me.
- Now I wonder why they are criticizing me? Perhaps they are feeling threatened?

Feelings

Feelings are inner experiences such as anger, boredom, happiness, worry, jealousy, excitement, satisfaction, guilt, fear and so on. They are important not only as inner experiences, some pleasant and some unpleasant, but also because they often affect the way we behave.

The relationship between feelings and behaviour is controversial. Some argue that feelings actually *cause* behaviour, others that behaviour causes feelings. Whatever the precise relationship, there is general agreement that both feelings and behaviours are reactions to some external event. We don't just feel angry, for example, in a vacuum – something happens to trigger it. It may be something someone does or says or it may be something happening, like being delayed in a traffic jam or missing a train it was important to catch.

The crucial difference between feelings and behaviour is that feelings are internal and cannot be observed by anyone else. If you express your feelings in your outward actions then it is the expression of them (in your behaviour) that is observed, *not* the feelings themselves. This difference between internal and external events has important implications. For example, you can never *know* how someone is feeling. You can only guess or infer it from your observations of their behaviour. Similarly, no-one else is able to access your feelings. They remain a private experience unless you choose to reveal them in your spoken or unspoken actions. By their very nature, therefore, feelings, unlike behaviour, are not susceptible to direct control by other people. You cannot control other people's feelings nor other people yours. Your feelings are entirely your own. Of course others may do their best to influence your feelings but, as we shall see, you and you alone choose whether to let this happen or not.

Feelings can be divided roughly into two categories:

- Feelings which help you to function effectively. An example would be having a level of anxiety that helps to lift your performance so that you do better than if you took things routinely in your stride.

- Feelings which hinder you from functioning as effectively as you are capable of doing. Feelings like anger, worry and guilt, for example, are only worth having if they help you to do something effective about the situation that is causing them. Unfortunately feelings like these often prevent you from taking effective action as well as being unpleasant while they last.

Clearly feelings that enhance your performance (ie outward behaviour) are splendid to have and enjoy. By contrast feelings that pull your performance down are both unwelcome and unpleasant. It is possible to learn how to prevent unproductive feelings (see *Preventing unwanted feelings* on page 138) but most people find this difficult to accept because they hold some erroneous beliefs about the nature of feelings. The four most common are:

That all feelings are instinctive rather than learned

Some internal experiences *are* instinctive in the sense that they were there from the word go, eg the sensation of the heart pounding and the adrenalin flowing when we are afraid. Instinctive sensations are built into the system and are triggered automatically in certain situations.

But the majority of the feelings we experience aren't instinctive at all. They have been acquired over a long period of *ad hoc* learning. You weren't born worrying or feeling guilty or bored. You weren't born feeling inadequate. These are feelings which develop as you are exposed to different experiences. Things happen and gradually you learn to associate external happenings with internal feelings. Eventually the learning is so thorough that it seems as though external events automatically trigger inner feelings. Take the feeling of jealousy for example. Studies show that people describe quite different emotional experiences under the general heading of jealousy. This suggests it comes in many different brands and sizes rather than being built into our innate system of reflexes, body chemistry, gene structure and the like. Furthermore, anthropological studies in cultures quite different from our own reveal that some cultures produce people who are entirely free of jealous feelings.

So there is evidence to suggest that many of our feelings are learned. This opens up the possibility of unlearning unproductive 'bad' feelings and replacing them with more productive 'good' ones.

Feelings cannot be controlled; they just happen to you

If you believe this it means you are a zombie with no responsibility for how you feel. You are completely at the mercy of other people and events and believe they are entirely to blame for your feelings. I challenge this depressing view by suggesting that if so many of our feelings have been acquired through a learning process then we can continue to learn, unlearn, adapt, modify, update, replace and do anything we like with them. Feelings, like behaviour, are amenable to modification and change.

Of course so many of your feelings are ingrained and habitual that you may not be aware that you can exercise choice. But, if you think about it, you'll realize:

- that your feelings don't just happen in a vacuum; they are always preceded by an external event and by a conscious thought.
- that you can choose what feelings to have in relation to an external event. No-one can *make* you feel anything emotionally. No-one, nor any event, can *make* you feel angry, for example. You can choose whether to *feel* angry in just the same way that you can choose whether to react angrily.

It takes practice to get the choice mechanisms working again. In most people they've lain idle for so long that it takes deliberate, conscious thought processes to stir them into action. (For more about how to do this see *Preventing unwanted feelings* on page 138.)

You should suppress your feelings

This suggests that inner feelings should be contained and not allowed to be reflected in outward actions. In our society this is a strongly held belief since many feelings (of hostility and aggression for example) are not considered desirable or civilized so we suppress them. But experiencing the feeling without expressing it puts undue stresses on the system that can eventually result in unwanted side-effects. Nervous breakdowns, ulcers, coronaries, headaches, backaches often result from intolerable stresses trapped between inner feelings and outward behaviour.

Clearly a much healthier option would be to prevent unwanted feelings (ie not to have them in the first place or to nip them in the bud) so that there is nothing to suppress.

You should openly express your feelings and to hell with the consequences

Applied indiscriminately this could get you into a lot of unnecessary trouble! This assumes that we have feelings that *must* be released through outward expression. It obviously isn't socially acceptable or expedient to let behaviour be entirely dictated by feelings which is why the suppression strategy is so widely adopted. Expressing feelings may well avoid the penalties of suppressing them but is likely to trigger adverse reactions in other people. You could even finish up in jail!

First impressions

First impressions are unique because you never get a second chance to make a first impression. First impressions are based on just two 'things':

- your appearance
- your behaviour.

First impressions are arrived at by comparing what someone looks like and how they conduct themselves against a purely subjective yardstick of likes and dislikes, biases and prejudices, in the eye of the beholder. First impressions are, therefore, frequently misleading but unfortunately tend to stick. Having formed a first impression, people will often confirm its validity by only noticing things which confirm it and conveniently ignoring things which refute it. In this way erroneous first impressions can remain stubbornly in place for long periods of time.

Care needs to be taken, therefore, to create a favourable first impression by both looking and behaving the part. The precise details of what is appropriate will depend, of course, on the part, but a 'middle of the road' appearance is less risky than anything that could be considered 'way out' and the *helpful behaviours* (see page 84) are also a safe bet.

When forming first impressions of other people, the best guide is to remind yourself that it is only a first impression and to force yourself to revise and update it in the light of fresh data. The trick is to resist the temptation to form too quick an impression, based purely on someone's appearance. It is better to postpone judgement until the person's appearance fades in significance and to pay careful attention to their behaviour, upon which it is safer to reach conclusions.

Flexibility

Most people, despite protestations to the contrary, stick to a fairly narrow band of behaviours. This is entirely understandable since repeating familiar, and previously sufficiently successful, behaviour patterns is far easier than constantly modifying your behaviour to suit differing circumstances. An argument frequently advanced for being consistent is that it is fairer on other people, they know what to expect and 'where they stand'. The alternative argument has it that since people and situations differ you are better equipped to deal with them if you have a wide repertoire of behaviours to draw on.

Oscillating between wild extremes of behaviour is interesting, but ill-advised and unnecessary. On the other hand being sufficiently flexible to make small adjustments to your behaviour, providing the chosen mode is appropriate, is likely to be effective. Everyone is able to choose how to behave in a given set of circumstances, although many people operate on the assumption that they cannot choose and never give the alternatives a moment's thought. You can choose, for example, whether to:

- talk or listen
- question or answer
- look at the person or look away
- be positive or negative
- be friendly or formal
- laugh or cry,

and so on.

These are all significantly different ways of behaving and they are open to everyone.

Varying your behaviour is fine, with two important provisos:

1 You need to be consistent within a single interaction. Chopping and changing your behaviour within a short space of time is likely to confuse and be unhelpful.
2 You need to be open about the way you have chosen to behave. Just a simple explanation will do, such as 'I've thought about this and decided that I'd better shut up and do most of the listening'. It is rare for such declarations to be made – but that is usually because people haven't given any thought as to how best to behave and therefore have nothing to declare.

Games

Games, in the special psychological sense in which the word is used in *transactional analysis* (see page 167), are closely allied to *strokes* and *discounts* (see pages 156 and 55). A game is basically a manoeuvre that people indulge in to get the strokes they need and/or to be in a position to discount others. A game always has at least one loser. Games are condemned in TA as damaging to authentic relationships between people, time-wasting and unproductive. Games are played by either the Parent or Child *ego-states* (see page 56) and are outside the awareness of the Adult. This means that on the surface the transactions may appear complementary but below the surface the rules of the particular game provide a *hidden agenda* (see page 85). The hidden agenda is called an ulterior transaction and is represented diagrammatically by dotted lines rather than the solid ones used to illustrate *complementary and crossed transactions* (see page 58).

On the following page are some examples of games played from the Child ego-state. On the surface transactions appear to involve an employee asking with his Adult for suggestions from his manager. And the manager, in turn, appears to be replying with ideas from his Adult. There is, however, a second, or hidden, psychological level of communication occurring. At this level the subordinate is saying 'I'm helpless to solve my own problems so I need a wise

Subordinate	*Manager*
1 'I really would like to get your help in solving my work overload problem.'	2 'Would it help if you planned more carefully? Perhaps a wall chart would help?'
3 'Yes but while I'm planning I could be getting on with one of the jobs.'	4 'Why not delegate more? Could Bill do more for example?'
5 'I've tried that but he is as overloaded as I am.'	6 (etc)

person (Parent) like you to solve them for me.' The manager, in turn, responds on the psychological level with: 'Yes I recognize my wisdom and will be happy to give you advice.' But then in the 3rd and 5th parts of the transaction, the employee rejects the advice that he appeared to be asking for.

If we look only at the surface of this transaction, it won't make sense to us. It appears contradictory that someone should ask for advice and then reject it. If, however, we look at the hidden psychological level, we can begin to see that the basic purpose of the transaction was to reject advice rather than to receive it. By rejecting the manager's ideas the subordinate is able 'to prove' his superiority over the boss in an underhanded or crooked way. Thus the subordinate finishes up feeling good and gives himself a stroke, the manager loses and collects a discount for his pains. This particular game is called 'Yes, but . . .' and is played from the Child ego-state. Other games played out of the Child ego-state are:

Kick me

The person repeatedly sets up situations so that they are caught and, figuratively, kicked as though a Kick Me sign were pinned on their back. The feelings he or she gets when 'kicked' are comfortingly familiar and better than being ignored.

See what you made me do?

An example of this would be a secretary who angrily snatches a piece of paper from the typewriter while shooting a glance at the manager who is standing too near for comfort. The crooked pay-off is that the secretary feels blameless and discounts the innocent manager.

Love me no matter what I do

Players of this game put out one 'bait' after another hoping that someone will tell them to stop it. When they do, they turn on the person and accuse him or her of being old-fashioned and not accepting them as they are.

Harried executive

Played by people who keep so busy with minute details that they always seem harassed. At first people respond to this sympathetically and avoid asking the person to do more. Eventually the player is likely to lose out, however, by getting a reputation for being disorganized.

In addition to the games played by the Child there are some played from the Parent ego-state. The ingredients are exactly the same – the game is essentially a crooked manoeuvre to get or give strokes and/or discounts. Here is an example:

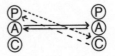

Manager	*Subordinate*
1 'Were you late again this morning?'	2 'I'm afraid I was.'
2 'Right! You've forced me to take some action . . . etc.'	

This is a trapping game called 'Now I've Got You'. The manager attempts to catch the subordinate making a mistake and this 'justifies' a discount. Discounts might be a sacking, disciplinary action, withholding a promotion or rise, writing a critical letter and so on.

Other games played out of the Parent ego-state are:

Blemish

This is played from the Critical Parent where someone is apparently praising a job well done but spoils the effect by pointing out a relatively insignificant imperfection. Pedantic people are prone to do this with minor typing errors or spelling mistakes.

I'm only trying to help you

This is played from the Nurturing Parent. In this game someone offers help even though it hasn't been requested. After they have put themselves out to help, the other person makes it clear that help wasn't wanted. The helper departs feeling 'put down' and badly done by.

Games always result in a win-lose outcome where someone comes out on top but at the other person's expense. The loser is likely to be tempted into playing a return game on some future occasion in a bid to square the match. This 'tit for tat' competition wastes time, saps energy and sours relationships.

How can we recognize when a game is being played? Here are some of the usual indicators. Ask yourself:

- Has this same pattern of events happened with this person before? (People have favourite games that are repetitious).
- Are the verbal and non-verbal messages in this person's behaviour consistent? (Non-verbal aspects are harder to control so they are often a 'window' on the ulterior transaction).
- Is what I'd expected to happen actually happening? (If it isn't, you are probably in a game).
- Do I feel bad, exploited, put down? Or, do I feel triumphant, the winner? (Games inevitably result in these feelings).

When you spot a game for what it is how can you stop it? Here are some useful ways:

- Go back to your Adult and try to hook the other person's Adult. (The Adult ego-state does not play games).
- Confront the game by finding some way to express the unexpectedness of the behaviour.
- Ignore the game and find some way of refusing to produce the complementary behaviour. (It takes two to play a game).

If you fail to recognize a game until it's too late what can you do to reduce the damage and learn from the experience?

- If you are the victim of a game refuse to take on the bad feeling it leaves you with. (See *Preventing unwanted feelings* on page 138).
- After a game, whether you were the winner or loser, use your Adult to ask yourself 'How did it start?' 'Did the game come from my Parent or Child?' 'What can I do to prevent its repetition?'

For other concepts from Transactional analysis see *Ego-states*, page 56, *Strokes*, page 156, *Discounts*, page 55, *OKness*, page 123.

Genuineness

Genuineness is a judgement people make based, as it must be, on the way you behave. People are likely to conclude that you are genuine if you do some or all of the following things:

- Ensure that your non-verbal behaviour matches what you are saying. For example, it isn't considered genuine to say 'How nice to see you' whilst rummaging through the contents of your in-tray.
- Openly admit to your own fallibility.
- Share your objectives with people.
- Share your feelings with people.

Whilst you might use these behaviours and through them create an impression of being genuine, it will, of course, quickly be destroyed unless you do what you say you will do. If for some reason it subsequently becomes obvious that you can't do what you said you'd do, then the genuine thing to do is to contact the person *before* the deadline expires, admit your difficulty and negotiate a new deadline.

Going round in circles

Meetings are infamous for getting stuck and going round in circles. In behavioural terms this usually occurs when people participating in the meeting get locked into an information loop. The loop goes like this:

Person A	Asks a question of clarification
Person B	Provides clarification
Person C	Provides clarification of the clarification
Person D	Adds some further information
Person E	Asks a question to elicit more information
Person D	Provides more information
Person C	Adds some further information
Person A	Asks a question of clarification
Person B	Provides clarification
and so on!	

Both information and clarification are essential in all meetings, indeed they are the essence of any communication between people. The problem of going round in circles is caused by a surplus of information and explanation, and a deficit of ideas and reactions to those ideas. The peril of getting caught in an information loop is made plain if we look at the following facts.

- Whenever you ask a question of clarification or ask for information nine times out of ten clarification or information is forthcoming.
- Whenever you give clarification or provide information four times out of ten someone else will follow you by doing the same and three times out of ten someone else will follow you by asking for more.
- This means that seven times out of ten the provision of clarification or information results in more of the same or requests for more.

- On average in a meeting, seeking clarification and giving clarification amount to 44 per cent of *all* the spoken behaviours.
- On average in a meeting there are two answers to every question (the actual figures are 15 per cent for seeking clarification and 29 per cent for giving clarification).

It is easy to see, therefore, how going round in circles is not a vicious circle, but a circle nonetheless. The reason why people prolong the information loop is because it is a relatively 'safe' way to pass the time. Exchanging information is not as risky as sticking your neck out by suggesting an idea, so people tend to prolong information-swopping and postpone idea-having.

The answer is to recognize that the conversation has got stuck in a circle and to take an initiative to break it. The most obvious initiatives are to seek an idea from someone or to put an idea yourself (see *Seeking ideas* on page 152 and *Idea-having* on page 86).

Groups

Groups, like the people that comprise them, come in different shapes and sizes. A group is a collection of individual people who come together to achieve some purpose. A group is a lesser thing than a team, which performs at a higher level of cohesion than a mere group needs to (see *Teams* on page 161).

Generally speaking, the more a group exceeds seven people the more cumbersome it becomes. This is because each individual brings a different mix of strengths and weaknesses, experiences and perceptions. On the one hand this provides an excellent opportunity for the group to tap into a wide diversity of views. On the other hand it makes it difficult to reach genuine agreement on anything at all. Sometimes agreement is apparent rather than real because of the tendency to conform and fall in with majority opinion. This results in the faint-hearted acquiescing (see *Acquiescence* on page 1).

Because of the difficulties of getting it all together, the chairperson or co-ordinator has a key part to play (see *Chairing meetings* on page 28). Unfortunately, most groups cannot boast a chairperson or co-ordinator who is up to the job. The most frequent reason is

that the chairperson gets too involved in the task and doesn't do
enough to manage the process.

To comprehend fully the distinction between task and process it
is necessary to appreciate the evolutionary stages that groups go
through:

Stage 1   *The chaotic stage*

Groups of people who are thrown together and given a task to
tackle tend to underestimate the complexities of getting a group to
cohere. This is especially true if the group starts from scratch with
no designated roles or previous experience of working together.

A group in the chaotic stage tries to overcome uncertainty and
ambiguity by flinging itself headlong into the task in hand without
giving enough, if any, attention to the process. The noticeable
characteristics of a group in the chaotic stage are:

- No time is given to setting clear objectives that everyone sub-
  scribes to. The group assumes that everyone knows what the
  objectives are.
- Inadequate time is given to planning how to tackle the task.
- If a leader is appointed, no thought is given to clarifying the
  leader's role; it is likely that the appointed leader will try to
  impose his or her authority on a group which will not consent.
- Ideas will be voiced but not listened to and developed; or
  rejected because the level of interrupting and overspeaking will
  be inefficiently high.
- The success of the group will be patchy; sometimes, despite the
  chaos, it will get by; sometimes it will fail. Whatever the outcome, the tendency to rationalize, ie for people to claim that
  they *did* achieve what they set out to, is high.

Stage 2 – *The formal stage*

Eventually a group will react against the chaotic stage by tightening
up and becoming more formal. It is very likely to over-react, however, and introduce formal procedures that swing the pendulum too
far the other way. The most noticeable characteristics of a group in
the formal stage are:

- There will be rigid, step by step, procedures for agreeing objectives and plans. Typically a group might have a system of going round the table, letting everyone have their say. It might also instigate a system of writing up the objective in large letters for all to see.

- The need for strong leadership is frequently emphasized. In a formal group this means ensuring that people stick to the procedures, don't argue, don't interrupt one another and so on. Strong leadership is seen as the solution to the problems of the chaotic stage. If the group fails, the leader is criticized for not being strong enough!

- Different people in the group will be given specific roles such as time keeper, secretary; and there will be explicit rules of behaviour such as only speaking through the chair, considering one idea at a time, recapping frequently from the secretary's minutes and so on.

- The success of the group will improve if the time limits are sufficiently elastic to allow extra time for all the formalities.

Stage 3 – The skilful stage

Gradually a group outlives the formal stage and begins to 'take liberties' with its own procedures without slipping back into chaos. Sometimes a group rebels against the rigidity of the formal stage too early and oscillates between the chaotic and formal stages. Sometimes a group gets stuck in the formal stage, convinced that formality and rules are the only antidote to chaos.

The breakthrough to the skilful stage usually occurs when the group realizes that some part of its formal procedures is inappropriate to the particular task in hand. It therefore cuts some corners and, in so doing, discovers that it can cope.

The most noticeable characteristics of a group in the skilful stage, ie a team, are:

- All procedures for objective setting, planning, time keeping or whatever are agreed in the light of the task to be done and the situation. The procedures are therefore flexible rather than rigid.

- The leader is less directive and more participative. Indeed, in a skilful team that has 'got it together', the role of leader is relatively redundant. A leader may just be needed occasionally as a 'long stop'. A formal-stage group is leader-dependent whereas a skilful-stage team is leader-independent.

- Team members, in whatever role, share equal responsibility for the success of the team.
- The atmosphere in the team is trusting and co-operative.
- The team is more successful in achieving challenging objectives.

One of the interesting discoveries about this evolutionary process is that a team operating at the skilful stage gets there via the formal stage. Just as only a caterpillar can become a butterfly, the formal stage seems a necessary developmental step to the skilful stage. The skills acquired from rigid planning are different in degree but not in kind from the skills required for flexible planning.

So the formal stage is an essential step in the learning process. It is the equivalent of learning to walk before you can run.

The secret of success is, therefore, to get a group into the formal stage as fast as possible. Once there, performance needs to be maintained by regular *reviews* (see page 147). If the group

- has sufficiently challenging tasks to tackle,
- has a reasonably constant core of members,
- is due to meet frequently (say, at least weekly),

then it may be appropriate for it to progress to operating at the skilful stage. For more on this, see *Teams* on page 161.

Guilt

Guilt is an unwanted feeling that frequently spills over into behaviour. Fortunately guilt is a preventable feeling but it is vital to read the section on *Preventing unwanted feelings* (on page 138) before reading the remainder of this section because what follows assumes you have understood the two options involved.

Unproductive guilt hinders your behaviour in a variety of ways. All or some of the following might apply to you:

- You waste time in the present lamenting over something that happened in the past.
- You say yes when you wanted to say no.
- You are a 'soft touch' and take the line of least resistance (ie 'tip'

someone even though you didn't want to, buy something you don't really want).

- You have an over-developed sense of duty and 'shoulds, oughts and musts' from the past compel you to serve other people/ become a do-gooder.
- You don't fully savour happy/frivolous moments because of a gnawing feeling that you ought to be doing something more worthwhile.
- You inflict your self-reproaches on people close to you.

Your guilt is always triggered by some external event or happening. Typical examples might be when:

- reminded of mistakes you made in the past – the sight/presence of someone you wronged in the past.
- someone close to you subjects you to emotional blackmail/puts pressure on you (ie 'It'll be your fault if I drop dead with a heart attack.' 'How can you treat me like this after all I have sacrificed for you?' 'All my friends are allowed to.').
- someone accuses you of embarrassing/boring/upsetting them ('Now see what you've made me do.').
- you do something you consider wrong or contrary to your self-imposed standards (ie letting someone down, pilfering, having an extra-marital affair, forgetting someone's birthday, being out at work when the children come home from school).
- you are rebuked by an 'authority figure' ('You should not/ought not/must not do so and so.').

Clearly, ideas for changing the events that trigger your guilt feelings will depend on the exact circumstances, but here are some thought-starters that might help you to arrive at a feasible plan:

- Keep a guilt diary. When does it happen? Doing what? With whom? Plan to avoid or minimize your exposure to guilt-provoking situations.
- The moment you are reminded of a past mistake say out loud 'That is past. I'll be careful not to repeat that mistake in the future.'
- When you consider you have wronged someone admit it and apologize. This cleans the slate making it less likely that you will

feel guilty or succumb to any future pressure or emotional blackmail.

- Write out your own personal ten commandments in the back of your diary (revise it each year) so that you are clear what your standards are. Check back whenever you are tempted to do something contrary to your commandments.
- Avoid people who pepper their conversation with 'shoulds, oughts and musts'.

Rather than modify anything to do with the external events that trigger your guilt you might decide to go for option 2 and identify the thoughts or beliefs that herald your guilt feelings and examine them for possible replacements. Typical thoughts for feelings of guilt are:

- I ought not to have done that.
- They are right – I deserve to feel ashamed of myself.
- Oh dear! I have upset them (as opposed to they are upset).
- I should not be doing this.
- It is all my fault.
- It is wrong to enjoy myself.

And, finally, here are some thought-starters on ways of replacing unrealistic thoughts and beliefs that provoke feelings of guilt so that they become more realistic and less likely to hinder your behaviour:

- The past is past and there is nothing I can do to change it.
- Nothing can make me feel guilty. I choose whether to feel guilty or not.
- Feeling guilty does not make me a better person.
- They are upset/annoyed/embarrassed but that is their choice.
- I've got just three choices:
    1 to stay and feel guilty
    2 to stay and enjoy it
    3 to get up and go
  One is daft, so shall I do two or three?
- I have a right to say no.

Habits

There are good habits and bad habits but the main point about them is that they are all behaviour patterns which have been so thoroughly learned that they are done automatically without any conscious effort. In fact if you concentrate attention on a habit it often causes the habitual behaviour pattern to break down. (Try thinking about your finger movements when you play a well-known tune on a keyboard – you make more mistakes than if you let your fingers do the thinking.)

Habitual behaviour patterns are, therefore, useful because they can be carried out effortlessly and free us to concentrate our energies on other things. The difficulty with habits is that they are difficult to change. Breaking a habit, be it over-eating, over-drinking, biting your nails or jumping to conclusions, is a tall order.

The key to success is to:

- Identify precisely *when* you indulge in the habit and what ingredients are present in the situation that triggers it. Then see what you can do to change the circumstances of the situation. So if, for example, you always smoke a cigarette when you have a cup of coffee, avoid drinking coffee.
- Replace the habit with something else rather than leaving a void. Clearly the replacement needs to be something desirable and/or less harmful than the original habit you are seeking to break. So, for example, it would be better to stick your head out of the window and take in six large gulps of air instead of smoking a cigarette than to cut out smoking and put nothing in its place.
- Reward yourself each time you succeed in breaking the habit. This acts as positive reinforcement. The rewards could be quick and simple such as reading the newspaper for five minutes, or having a quick chat on the phone with a friend.

These three actions are vastly superior to breaking a habit by will-power alone. Will-power is where you stop a habit without changing the situation (ie you still drink coffee), or replacing the habit with another activity or rewarding yourself. Not surprisingly will-power has a poor track record when it comes to permanently breaking entrenched behaviour patterns. (For more on behaviour change see *Behaviour modification* on page 16.)

Helpful behaviour

To some extent what constitutes a helpful and what constitutes an unhelpful behaviour is in the eye of the beholder (see *Customer satisfaction* on page 46). However, there are certain behaviours that more often than not are considered helpful and therefore tend to engender favourable reactions in the people you have dealings with. This applies whoever they are – senior to you, junior to you, same level as you, customers, acquaintances, friends, neighbours, relatives and members of your immediate family. Here is a list of 19 helpful behaviours that have been carefully researched.

- Lean forward with hands open, arms uncrossed and legs uncrossed
- Look at the other person for approximately 60 per cent of the time
- When listening, nod and make 'I'm listening' noises such as 'um', 'yes', 'really'
- Smile
- Sit beside the other person or if this isn't possible, at a 90 degree angle to them
- Use the other person's name early on in the transaction
- Ask the other person open questions
- Summarize back to the other person what you think they have said
- Say things that refer back to what the other person has said
- Show empathy by saying you understand how the other person feels and can see things from their point of view
- When in agreement with the other person, openly say so and say why
- Build on the other person's ideas
- Be non-judgemental towards the other person
- If you *have* to disagree with the other person, give the reason first then say you disagree
- Admit it when you don't know the answer or have made a mistake

- Openly explain what you are doing, or intending to do, for the other person
- Be genuine, with visual and verbal behaviours telling the same story
- Whenever possible, touch the other person
- Give the other person something, even if it is only a name card, or piece of paper with notes on it.

Hidden agendas

A hidden agenda is where someone's behaviour is determined by a motive which is undeclared and being deliberately concealed. A good example is where someone may question you about a situation ostensibly to become clearer about the facts. Unbeknown to you the real motive is to question you in order to undermine your position. Another famous one is where someone may come to you with a problem ostensibly to enlist your help in solving it. In fact they are out to prove that their problem is insoluble and that you couldn't help them.

These are both rather ominous examples of hidden agendas, because the reason for being secretive is because the real motive is essentially manipulative. Sometimes there is a hidden agenda which is more innocent where, for example, someone may question you about something in order to establish your credibility or in order to weigh you up.

Hidden agendas, precisely because they are under cover, are often difficult to detect. It usually dawns on you slowly that all is not as it would appear on the surface. The best antidote against hidden agendas is to insist on clarifying and agreeing a clear objective (see *Objectives* on page 119) before proceeding. Even this may still leave some hidden agendas lurking beneath the surface. The answer then is openly to confront the issue as soon as your suspicions are aroused. For further advice on tactics for avoiding hidden agendas or surfacing them, see *Games* on page 71.

Humour

Humour can be an excellent behaviour for easing tensions and breaking the ice between people. However, to achieve these objectives it needs to be:

- situational humour, ie funny within the context of the situation people are in at the time so that people can relate to it through a common, shared experience
- non-threatening, ie the humour is not at someone else's expense and does not ridicule anyone except yourself
- non-offensive to the people present, ie not sexist or racist or shockingly 'blue'
- spontaneous. If you succumb to the temptation to tell contrived jokes, ration yourself to two per day. This is because joke after joke is tedious and people quickly reach saturation point.

Idea-having

There are two distinct phases in having an idea. First you have to think of it and secondly you have to say it. Unfortunately, there are many people who think of ideas but, for various reasons, don't voice them. Often they fear ridicule or a rebuttal. At other times they lack the skills of assertion (see *Assertiveness* on page 8) and sometimes the gestation period is too long and the moment has passed. Producing off-the-top-of-the-head ideas (see *Creative thinking* on page 41) is particularly difficult for many people, especially those who feel vulnerable unless they have had time to prepare their idea carefully before offering it.

An idea is a possible course of action. if, for example you said 'It's 11 o'clock. Let's have a break for coffee', that would be an idea. If, however, you said 'It's 11 o'clock', that would *not* be an idea. It would only be a piece of information. If you said 'It's 11 o'clock. People often have a cup of coffee at this time', that would not be an idea either because it doesn't contain a sufficiently explicit course of action. Admittedly the action is heavily implied and most people would take the hint but the point is that, strictly speaking, ideas have to be explicit. Innuendos and hints do not count.

There are two different ways to voice an idea. You can propose it or suggest it. Proposed ideas are always statements such as 'It's 11 o'clock. We will break for coffee.' Suggestions are always questions such as 'It's 11 o'clock, shall we break for coffee?'

Remarkably this subtle difference in the way an idea is put makes a significant difference to the response. The facts are that if you propose an idea, four times out of ten someone will take issue with it by pointing out snags and difficulties (see *Difficulty stating* on page 52). If, on the other hand, you suggest an idea, four times out of ten someone will agree with it. The actual figures are:

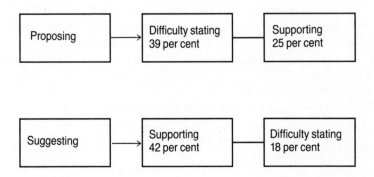

These data clearly indicate that 'suggesting', the more involving way of idea-having, is far more likely to win support. Despite this, most people persist in proposing their ideas at least twice as often as they suggest them!

If you aren't very good at thinking of ideas, try using other people's ideas as a springboard for your own. You can do this in a couple of ways. Whenever someone voices an idea, ie a possible course of action, analyse it by asking yourself 'What is wrong with that?' When you have thought of a snag either:

- think of an alternative idea that overcomes the snag
  or
- think of an addition to the other person's idea that improves it and overcomes the snag you have identified.

The latter alternative is preferable since it is more likely to be seen as constructive and thus win support (see *Building* on page 25). However, both tactics are ways of using other people's ideas as a stimulus for producing ideas yourself.

Idea-having is the best antidote to the common problem of going round in circles (see *Going round in circles* on page 76).

Inadequacy

Inadequacy is an unwanted feeling that frequently spills over into behaviour. Fortunately inadequacy is a preventable feeling but it is vital to read the section on *Preventing unwanted feelings* (on page 138) before reading the remainder of this section because what follows assumes you have understood the two options involved.

Unproductive feelings of inadequacy hinder your behaviour in a variety of ways. All or some of the following might apply to you:

- You crave constant approval/support/reassurance.
- You are non-assertive (ie hold back from giving your opinions, modify your stance to gain approval, agree with other people even when you don't).
- You are over-polite/over-apologetic/over-subservient.
- You constantly discount yourself: 'My opinion may not be worth much but . . .' 'I'm no good at this.' 'I'm sure you'll find fault with this.'
- You become embarrassed when people compliment you: 'Oh it was nothing really'.
- You never go out on a limb and try something new or different.
- You don't stand up straight, look people in the eye, shake hands firmly or leave decisively when it's time to go.
- You always think of the clever remark you could have made afterwards when it's too late.

Your feelings of inadequacy are always triggered by some external event or happening. Typical examples might be when:

- in the presence of people you regard as better looking/cleverer/ more accomplished than you
- you encounter someone who is good at something you are poor

at but aspire to (ie flirting, dancing, doing crossword puzzles, playing a musical instrument, telling jokes, playing sports, doing the Rubik cube in 38 seconds)

- you lose an intellectual argument because you weren't fast enough on your feet
- you fail (ie a test, exam, to get a job you applied for, to get the partner you wanted)
- you are abroad and can't speak the language
- you read the *Guinness Book of Records* or watch 'Mastermind' on TV or can't do your children's homework or lose at 'Trivial Pursuit'.

Clearly, ideas for changing the events that trigger your feelings of inadequacy will depend on the exact circumstances, but here are some thought-starters that might help you to arrive at a feasible plan:

- Avoid people who you think are better looking/cleverer/more accomplished than you.
- Choose an obscure subject/hobby and become a world authority on it.
- Learn a party piece and practise it till you can do it perfectly (ie a series of jokes, a juggling/conjuring trick, a puzzle that no-one can ever solve).
- Select one topical current affairs issue each week and swot up on it from newspapers and magazines. It is even more impressive if you can memorize some relevant statistics/figures.
- Take yourself in hand. Get fit, get slim, practise standing up straight with your hands behind your back (a sign of confidence).
- Force yourself to compliment/congratulate other people on their appearance/accomplishments. This gets you to concentrate on them rather than yourself and you'll discover that even the most famous people value your compliments.

Rather than modify anything to do with the external events that trigger your inadequacy, you might decide to go for option 2 and identify the thoughts or beliefs that herald your feelings of inadequacy and examine them for possible replacements. Typical thoughts for feelings of inadequacy are:

- I'm stupid/ugly/no good/a failure.

- I look silly.
- They are better than me.
- They can't possibly find me interesting.
- They are bound to expose my inadequacy.
- I need their approval.

And, finally, here are some thought-starters on ways of replacing unrealistic thoughts and beliefs that provoke feelings of inadequacy so that they become more realistic and less likely to hinder your behaviour:

- There are plenty of things I can do really well.
- Even if they think I'm silly, I'm not.
- They are better than me at some things. I am better than them at other things.
- If they don't find me interesting that's their loss.
- I decide whether to feel inadequate or not.
- As far as I am concerned no-one in the world is more important than me.

Influencing

Influencing is what behaviour is all about. Whenever you are interacting with someone you are to a greater or lesser extent trying to influence them. You might be trying to do this via their thoughts, beliefs, attitudes, feelings or by directly attempting to influence their behaviour.

As you might expect, some behaviours are more influential than others but *all* behaviours have a direct impact on other people. This is because all behaviours, spoken and unspoken, are overt and manifest. For details of the impact of *non-verbal behaviours* see page 116. For details of the impact of *verbal behaviours* see page 170. For further advice on how to be influential see *Persuasiveness* on page 128.

Inhibition

Inhibition is an unwanted feeling that frequently spills over into behaviour. Fortunately inhibition is a preventable feeling but it is vital to read the section on *Preventing unwanted feelings* (on page 138) before reading the remainder of this section because what follows assumes you have understood the two options involved.

Unproductive feelings of inhibition hinder your behaviour in a variety of ways. All or some of the following might apply to you:

- You are cautious/play it safe/hold back/don't experiment for fear of making a mistake/failing/looking stupid.
- You stick to the tried and true, never going at risk and trying something new/different. You resist change (ie travel the same way to work, read the same newspaper, wear the same sort of clothes, have fixed routines/habits, stick to familiar foods, stick to the same circle of friends).
- You can't be spontaneous or produce off-the-top-of-the-head ideas.
- You are unable to suspend judgement and dismiss/criticize activities you have never tried (ie yoga, jogging, ski-ing, hang-gliding).
- You turn down invitations to anything off-beat.
- You can't look someone in the eye and say 'I love you'.

Your feelings of inhibition are always triggered by some external event or happening. Typical examples might be when:

- you are a newcomer to a group
- you have to speak before a group
- you are in strange, unfamiliar surroundings/meeting strangers
- you meet people who are better looking/more accomplished than you
- someone invites you to a party or to try something new/different
- you feel exposed/that you might make a fool of yourself in front of others
- you realize you hold substantially different views to anyone else present
- getting undressed in front of someone else.

Clearly, ideas for changing the events that trigger your feelings of inhibition will depend on the exact circumstances, but here are some thought-starters that might help you to arrive at a feasible plan:

- Keep an inhibition log noting precisely what events inhibit you, then plan to avoid them.
- When you are a newcomer to a group take a friend you know well along with you.
- Prepare some opening gambits/topics you can use when first meeting strangers.
- Draw up a list of 20 things you have never done that are silly but don't cost much money and work your way down the list by doing one each day (eg leave your car in the garage and hitch a lift, turn the daily newspaper into papier mâché, go to the shops wearing a funny hat, shake hands with the next 10 people you meet).
- Make friends with someone who finds it easy to be spontaneous. Tag along with them, do what they do.
- Force yourself to initiate a conversation lasting at least five minutes with a stranger every other day.
- Brief people close to you to cajole you into doing things and not to take no for an answer.
- Go to an event where you will be 'forced' to join in (ie a barn dance with a persuasive caller, an evening at a bowling alley, a table-tennis competition).

Rather than modify anything to do with the external events that trigger your inhibition you might decide to go for option 2 and identify the thoughts or beliefs that herald your inhibition and examine them for possible replacements. Typical thoughts for feelings of inhibition are:

- I'll look stupid.
- I'm not sure what is going to happen.
- I may not like it.
- Will they approve of me?
- They'll see my faults and then they won't like me anymore.
- I know I won't be any good at this – they'll just laugh at me.

And, finally, here are some thought-starters on ways of replacing unrealistic thoughts and beliefs that provoke feelings of inhibition so that they become more realistic and less likely to hinder your behaviour:

- I may make a mess of this but that doesn't mean I'm stupid.
- Everyone makes mistakes.

- I may not like this, but I won't know unless I try it first.
- I don't *need* their approval.
- If they can't accept me as I am, good riddance.
- It's nice to amuse people.
- If I do this what is the *worst thing* that could happen to me?
- Nothing can make me feel inhibited – I decide whether to feel inhibited or not.
- Oh, what the hell . . . nothing ventured, nothing gained!

Instincts

Instincts are behaviours that you don't have to learn. They are reflexes built into the system from the word go. New-born babies don't have to learn to breathe, cry or suck and there are many other examples of similar 'survival' reflexes. An obvious difference between human beings and other animals is the relatively small number of behaviours that are instinctive to humans and the vast number of behaviours that are acquired through a process of learning. With animals it tends to be the other way round: more instinctive behaviour patterns and relatively less to learn.

The interesting question when it comes to human behaviour is how much to attribute to inheritance, both in the form of instincts and in predispositions to behave in certain ways, and how much to learning. This is known as the nature nurture controversy.

After 80 years of argument and counter argument there is no conclusive answer to the question nor is there ever likely to be one. For practical purposes it is probably safe to assume something like a 50/50 split and this is probably putting inherited factors too high. Even if we assume a 50/50 split that means a lot of our behaviour is learned and pliable. Thus we can, if we choose, unlearn and relearn ways of behaving rather than assuming it is something totally rigid and fixed.

For further discussion on this see *Personality* on page 127 and *Learning from experience* on page 100.

Integrity

See *Openness* on pages 126–127

Interpersonal skills

Interpersonal skills are behaviours, used face-to-face, that succeed in helping progress towards a useful outcome. That's a bit of a mouthful so let's separate the ingredients and examine them more carefully.

Behaviours (see page 13) are everything you say and do. They are important because they are so immediately apparent to everyone you come face-to-face with and therefore have a direct effect on other people.

Face-to-face (see page 61) covers a whole multitude of different interactions between people. It might be an informal chat with someone or it might be a formal meeting with a group of people. The point is that it is only during face-to-face encounters that your behaviour is totally evident. During 'phone calls, by contrast, only what you *say* counts. Written communications are different because whilst what you write represents your behaviour even though you are not present, it isn't happening 'in flight' as do face-to-face behaviours.

A useful outcome is the third ingredient, for what would be the point of skills that led you to a useless outcome? The proof of the pudding is in the eating, and the proof of people skills is that they make it as likely as possible that we achieve our objectives with people.

The trick is to get all three ingredients to come together in a smooth and easy symmetry. Face-to-face situations provide the context, objectives spell out the desirable end and behaviours are the means.

There are just six fundamental interpersonal skills which give us a process that is equally applicable in all situations. This is preferable to having a 'shopping list' of skills where the items on the list will inevitably vary in importance depending upon the situation. If, for example, you are discussing how to solve a problem with a person who has more experience than you, then listening would be high on your list. If, on the other hand, you knew much more about what had to be done to solve the problem than the other person, then communicating clearly and testing the other person's understanding would be higher priorities.

We avoid this 'it all depends' qualification if we have a few fundamental skills that apply in *all* situations. They are:

1 Analysing the situation
2 Establishing a realistic objective
3 Selecting appropriate ways of behaving
4 Controlling our behaviour
5 Shaping other people's behaviour
6 Monitoring our own and others' behaviour.

The first three skills are essentially about thinking, the last three are about doing. It is the combination of both that is vital, for there is no point in thinking without doing, nor in doing without thinking.

Notice also how these skills provide us with a timeless wisdom, applicable to all people-situations anywhere. Analysing the situation helps us to detect the circumstances that need to be heeded when setting an objective that is realistic. The objective, in turn, provides a backcloth against which to make choices about how best to behave. Each thinking skill cascades into the next and the three combined help us to be aware of the situation and to have worked out what to do about it. By consciously controlling our behaviour we are more likely to do things that need to be done to achieve the objective. In so doing we influence other people's behaviour in the only way possible – via our own behaviour. And all the while we monitor to keep tabs on what is happening and to get the feedback we need to make in-flight adjustments.

There is no doubt that improving your interpersonal skills by extending your repertoire of behaviours is not easy. As with the acquisition of any skill it requires conscious effort as each skill is practised to the point where it becomes effortless (see *Skilful behaviour* on page 155). Since an investment of time and effort is required it is important to be sure that it will all be worthwhile. Some of the advantages of improved interpersonal skills are that you will be better at:

- quickly assessing and understanding face-to-face situations. You will thus benefit from fewer misunderstandings
- setting specific and realistic objectives for face-to-face encounters with people. You will thus benefit from being clear in what you are aiming at and successfully achieving it more often than not

- choosing and using behaviours that complement the circumstances and are appropriate to the objective. You will thus benefit by having an easier, and pleasanter, interaction *en route* to achieving your objective
- being aware of other people's behaviour and influencing it. You will thus benefit from being able to use your own behaviour as a powerful influence.

These are just some of the potential benefits of enhanced interpersonal skills. Of course, you will have already acquired some people skills through an *ad hoc* process of learning from experience. There will undoubtedly be things you already do well, that no longer require any conscious effort on your part. The problem is that, quite understandably, we all tend to stick to the tried and true and therefore repeat over and over again the same skills. In effect, therefore, we stop acquiring any new skills and this may mean we risk having too narrow a repertoire of skills to equip us adequately for the variety of people-situations we are likely to encounter.

For further details on how to enhance your interpersonal skills see the following sections (preferably in this order): *Face-to-face situations*, page 61, *Objectives*, page 119, *Categories of behaviour*, page 26, *Verbal behaviour*, page 170, *Non-verbal behaviour*, page 116.

Interpreting behaviour
See *Observing behaviour* on pages 122–123

Interviewing

Interviewing is a special face to face encounter which comes in a number of different guises. There are selection interviews, exit interviews, disciplinary interviews, as well as interviews to discover people's opinions on everything from products to politics. Whatever the type of interview the basic purpose is always the same: to elicit information from the interviewee.

The key skills of interviewers are all included in different sections of this book. They are:

- Being clear on your objectives (see *Objectives* on page 119).
- Planning your behaviour (see *Planning behaviour* on page 131).
- Establishing rapport (see *Rapport* on page 144).
- Asking questions (see *Asking questions* on page 8).
- Summarizing (see *Summarizing* on page 159).

One of the hazards of interviewing is succumbing to the temptation of jumping to a conclusion too quickly, based perhaps on a hastily formed first impression (see *First impressions* on page 69). It helps to counteract this tendency if you have a clear list of criteria against which to view the person and/or the information the interview renders.

Jealousy

Jealousy is an unwanted feeling that frequently spills over into behaviour. Fortunately jealousy is a preventable feeling but it is vital to read the section on *Preventing unwanted feelings* (on page 138) before reading the remainder of this section because what follows assumes you have understood the two options involved.

Unproductive feelings of jealousy hinder your behaviour in a variety of ways. All or some of the following might apply to you:

- You sulk/maintain a stony silence.
- You become vicious/spiteful/sarcastic/violent.
- You become suspicious/distrustful/watchful/keep checking up/ relentlessly supervise.
- You seek to maintain control over people important to you (ie you restrict their freedom, lay down rigid rules, issue ultimatums, become possessive/unreasonable).
- You become hostile/competitive towards real or imagined rivals.
- You constantly seek reassurance: 'You do love me don't you?' 'You will never leave me will you?'
- You threaten to commit suicide.

Your jealousy is always triggered by some external event or happening. Typical examples might be when:

- your partner talks with old friends about things you don't know about
- someone you know (friend, neighbour, colleague) succeeds at something you aspire to
- your partner tells you about the good times he/she had before meeting you
- your partner talks about his/her work or an interest that you can't understand or join in
- everyone clusters appreciatively round your partner at a party and ignores you
- your partner flirts with/has an affair with someone else
- you lose control over your partner (ie they insist on pursuing a time-consuming interest that excludes you, they go off and do their own thing).

Clearly, ideas for changing the events that trigger your jealousy will depend on the exact circumstances, but here are some thought-starters that might help you to arrive at a feasible plan:

- Choose friends/partners who aren't as accomplished as you are.
- Avoid ambiguous situations that you can't control.
- Keep busy! Have lots of engrossing things you can fall to doing if you are abandoned.
- When your partner talks about things you don't know about, bombard him/her with questions. This stops you being excluded.
- Draw up a 'contract' with your partner spelling out the limits of acceptable behaviour. It helps if you both keep independent jealousy logs for a few weeks beforehand. Then you find out what needs to go into the 'contract'.

Rather than modify anything to do with the external events that trigger your jealousy you might decide to go for option 2 and identify the thoughts or beliefs that herald your jealousy and examine them for possible replacements. Typical thoughts for feelings of jealousy are:

- They are enjoying themselves – I am being excluded/rejected/abandoned/ignored.
- I can no longer thrill, dazzle, charm or delight. There must be something wrong with me.

- He/she thinks they are more attractive/better than me. I may lose them and that would be *terrible*!
- He/she will compare me with them and find me wanting.
- Why are they doing this to me? I knew he/she couldn't be trusted.
- I can't survive without them.
- Lucky them – poor me!

And, finally, here are some thought-starters on ways of replacing unrealistic thoughts and beliefs that provoke feelings of jealousy so that they become more realistic and less likely to hinder your behaviour:

- They are enjoying themselves but that takes nothing away from me.
- No-one can make me feel jealous. I choose to feel jealous.
- I don't like it – but I can lump it!
- This isn't catastrophic or awful or terrible. It is just annoying/ irritating/disappointing/unfortunate.
- The only person I possess is me.
- I don't depend on *them*. I depend on *me*.

Leadership

Opinions vary as to what a leader really is. It is helpful to think of a leader more as a role with characteristic ways of behaving than as a particular person. Usually organizations and groups have designated leaders but even then it doesn't necessarily follow that the official leader will behave as such. If you examine the way people are behaving you may discover that someone else is acting as unofficial leader. Often the role is shared, with different people at different times doing the leading.

An effective leader is concerned both with the task in hand (the 'what') and with the decision-making processes (the 'how'). It is the role of a leader to:

- create the rules for others to follow
- take risks and make 'exposed' decisions which go outside existing or accepted constraints
- wrestle with ambiguity and uncertainty (rule making is always a

messier, more uncertain process than rule following)
- enthusiastically communicate a vision to people (vision is seeing the cathedral while you're mixing the cement)
- bounce back when things go wrong and find new pathways, blaze new trails.

A leader can only achieve results through other people and in doing so needs to draw on a range of different styles such as *Directive* (see page 53), *Consultative* (see page 38), *Collaborative* (see page 32), and *Delegation* (see page 49). The acid test of a good leader is the extent to which they select a style to suit the circumstances.

Learning from experience

Learning from experience is such a fundamental process that it is easy to take it for granted and assume that having experiences and learning from them are synonymous. But is it true that we learn just by virtue of being busy and having lots of experiences? Clearly *something* rubs off because you can observe people developing habits and behaviour patterns as a direct result of repetition. This is an example of learning to cope.

However, learning to cope is only a fraction of what is involved in learning from experience. What about learning how to change things for the better rather than merely learning to adapt to the way things are now? Learning to cope is a recipe for *complacency* (see page 35). Learning from experience is a recipe for continuous improvement.

Learning from experience is a process and, like all processes, it is possible to break it down into its constituent parts.

Stage 1: Having an experience

Clearly, it is difficult to learn from experience if you don't have any. Fortunately, most people have plenty of experiences. However, there are two different ways of having an experience. One is to let the experience come to you (reactive) and the other, to deliberately seek it out (proactive). The opportunities to learn from experience are greatly increased if the normal everyday things which happen to you are supplemented by extra experiences that you create. Suppose, for example, you regularly attend a weekly meeting which tends to be deadly dull. As a learner from experience you could decide to view it as a learning opportunity and start to experiment with different ways of running the meeting.

Stage 2: Reviewing the experience

If we are to learn from an experience it is vital to review what happened during the experience. Unfortunately, in the hurly-burly of a busy existence it is likely that the next experience will occur (rather like waves relentlessly breaking on the shore) before there has been time to review.

Reviewing involves looking back over what happened during the experience in a non-judgemental way. Once you are in the habit of reviewing it can be done, alone or with others who participated in the experience, in about five minutes flat.

To return to the example of the deadly dull meeting. You might have experimented by having a different person take the chair for different agenda items. In this case your review might focus on the differences you had observed between the way the best and worst chairperson had undertaken the task.

Stage 3: Concluding from the experience

Clearly there would be little point in reviewing the experience unless it helped you to reach some conclusions. The temptation is to jump to conclusions without arriving at them via a review. Unfortunately jumping to conclusions as a practice has a poor track record since, so frequently, they are proved to be inadequate or wrong.

Concluding involves scanning the raw material from the review for conclusions, 'answers' or lessons learned. There is no limit to the number or variety of different conclusions that can be reached at this stage in the process. It helps, though, if the conclusions are specific rather than global or 'motherhood'.

To return once again to the example of the meeting. You might conclude from your review of the styles of the best and worst chairperson that the best one:

- clarified the objective of whatever was to be discussed
- actively sought people's ideas
- summarized at frequent intervals.

Stage 4: Planning the next steps

There is little point in reaching conclusions unless you do something better or differently as a result. Before being in a position to do that, you need a plan. The peril is that intentions will be mistaken for plans and thus not be in a sufficiently doable form.

Planning involves translating at least some of the conclusions into a form where they can be put into action when next it is appropriate to do so. An example of a plan resulting from the conclusions about the key differences between the best and worst chairperson might be to spend 10 minutes at the start of the next meeting discussing your conclusions and working out how to give those who had most difficulty with the three modes of behaviour most practice, encouragement and feedback.

The four stages in the process of learning from experience are therefore mutually dependent on one another. No stage makes sense, or is particularly useful, in isolation from the others. The whole process can be summarized in a simple diagram which looks like this:

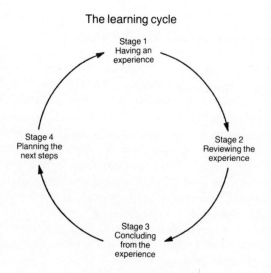

The learning cycle

Stage 1
Having an
experience

Stage 2
Reviewing the
experience

Stage 3
Concluding
from the
experience

Stage 4
Planning the
next steps

As you look at the above diagram of the learning cycle you may well be saying to yourself 'Is that all there is to it? Why, I do that already!' I venture to suggest, however, that you are probably, in common with most people, doing *some* parts of the process but not all of it. This is because you will have developed, without necessarily ever having thought about it, some learning style preferences that equip you better for certain stages in the cycle than for others.

Essentially there are four different learning styles:

Activist: 'I'll try anything once'
Reflector: 'I'd like time to think about this'
Theorist: 'How does this fit with that?'
Pragmatist: 'How can I apply this in practice?'

Each style equips you to carry out a different stage in the learning cycle. Activist tendencies aid and abet stage 1, having experiences; Reflector tendencies stage 2, reviewing; Theorist tendencies stage 3, concluding; Pragmatist tendencies stage 4, planning. Having all four styles comfortably within your repertoire thus equips you best for the total process of learning from experience. Unfortunately researches show that only two per cent of people are in this category and, therefore, qualify as 'all round' learners. You are more likely to be amongst the 35 per cent who only have one preference, or the 24 per cent who have two preferences, or the 20 per cent who have three preferences. (In case you are wondering about the arithmetic, 19 per cent don't have any preferences at all!)

The best way to ensure you learn from experience is to adopt a discipline which forces you to complete all the stages in the learning cycle. This can be done by regularly keeping a written learning log. It takes about 15 minutes to do this so you will have to be realistic about how frequently you could schedule it in. Even once a week would be better than nothing. Three times a week would be admirable. The learning log routine is simple:

- Start by thinking back over the experience and selecting a part of it (a 15 minute period or so) which was significant or important to you.
- Write a detailed account of what happened during that period of the activity. Don't at this stage put any effort into deciding what you learned – just concentrate on describing what actually happened.
- List the conclusions you have reached as a result of the experience. These are, in effect, your learning points. Don't limit the

number and don't worry about the practicality or quality of the
points.
- Finally, decide which learning points you want to implement in
  the future and work out an action plan which covers:

> What you are going to do
> When you are going to do it.

> Spell out your action plan as precisely as possible so that you are
> clear what you have to do and that it is realistic.

The advantage of this self-imposed discipline is that it forces you
deliberately to do all that is involved in learning from experience
and at the same time markedly increases the lessons learned from
your various activities.

The original Henry Ford said 'Anyone who stops learning is old,
whether at 20 or 80. Anyone who keeps learning stays young. The
greatest thing in life is to keep your mind young.' If learning from
experience can do that it must be a good thing!

Manipulation

Manipulation can be considered good or bad depending on the
context in which it is used. It is generally considered good to
manipulate the controls of a machine but bad to manipulate election
results. It is good to manipulate a strained back but bad to manipulate the market. On the one hand manipulation means to handle
something with skill and on the other to make dishonest changes to
suit your purpose.

Manipulating people by tricking them into doing something
which is against their best interests is clearly bad. By contrast,
interpersonal skills encourage people to achieve their objectives by
being honest and open rather than dishonest and furtive.

Manipulating behaviour is usually considered bad but this is
more debatable. Many people feel that behaviour should be
'natural' (see page 113) and spontaneous rather than premeditated
and planned. The assumption is that natural behaviour is honest
and planned behaviour is dishonest. The irony is that the more
people are encouraged to think about their behaviour and take
responsibility for the impact it has on other people, the more they

tend to become open and honest rather than furtive and clandestine. Thinking about behaviour and its likely effects are prerequisites for considerate, helpful behaviour. Few people regard considerate behaviour as in any way manipulative.

People often feel that it is in some way distasteful deliberately to use your behaviour to influence others and this also leads to the conclusion that manipulating behaviour is unethical. The plain fact is, however, that behaviour, whether it is deliberate or not, *always* influences people. This being so, it is surely better to acknowledge the power of behaviour and use it to *improve* relationships and enhance communication between people.

Behaviour can help or hinder just like a hammer that can be used to construct or destroy. The gamble is that the more people know about the workings of behaviour the more they will use it skilfully to benefit themselves and others. The choice, as always, is yours. See *Helpful behaviour* on page 84 and *Unhelpful behaviour* on page 169.

Meditation

There are various meditation or relaxation techniques which are admirable in counteracting the effects of stress and in releasing unwanted feelings (see *Preventing unwanted feelings* on page 138). If you use a meditation technique regularly it helps you to acquire a calm frame of mind so that you are not so vulnerable to the onset of unproductive feelings.

Experiments have shown that many relaxation techniques result in a state of consciousness quite unlike either being awake or being asleep. The state has been described as one of 'restful alertness' and physiological measures have shown that the heart rate decreases, metabolism is lowered, breathing rate decreases, blood pressure is lowered and brain waves change pattern.

There are four basic components necessary to successful meditation.

- A quiet environment
- A mental device, usually a sound, word or phrase repeated silently to help break the train of distracting thoughts
- A passive attitude. Adopt a 'let it happen' attitude. Distracting thoughts will occur but do not worry about them. Also don't worry about how well you are performing the technique. The

passive attitude is perhaps the most important element in successful meditation.

- A comfortable position, usually sitting down in a chair with no undue muscular tension. It is best *not* to lie down since this makes it easy to fall asleep. (Sleeping is not meditating!)

The most straightforward meditation/relaxation technique (there are many different permutations) is as follows:

1 Sit quietly in a comfortable position.
2 Close your eyes.
3 Deeply relax all your muscles, beginning at your feet and progressing up to your face. Keep them relaxed.
4 Breathe through your nose. Become aware of your breathing. As you breathe out, say the word 'one' silently to yourself. For example, breathe in . . . out, 'one'; in . . . out, 'one' etc. Breathe easily and naturally.
5 Continue for 10 to 20 minutes. You may open your eyes to check the time, but do not use an alarm. When you finish, sit quietly for several moments, at first with your eyes closed and later with your eyes opened. Do not stand up for a few moments.
6 Do not worry about whether you are successful in achieving a deep level of relaxation. Maintain a passive attitude and permit relaxation to occur at its own pace. When distracting thoughts occur, try to ignore them by not dwelling on them and return to repeating 'one'. With practice relaxation should come effortlessly. Practise the technique once or twice daily, but not within two hours after any meal, since the digestive processes seem to interfere with meditation.

Meetings

Meetings are infamous for taking up time when people claim they would otherwise be doing 'proper' work. Meetings are, of course, an important part of work; indeed some people have calculated that they spend at least 60 per cent of their time in meetings of one sort or another.

Meetings are not just time-consuming they are also expensive. If you calculate the cost of people's salaries, travelling expenses involved in getting to and from the meeting place etc it can come to a frightening figure per hour's worth of meeting.

There are a number of reasons why meetings tend to have a poor reputation. Amongst them are:

- a lack of clear purpose or objective
- poor chairmanship
- the wrong people at the meeting
- behavioural problems such as getting side-tracked, going round in circles, people hogging it
- interruptions through messages and phone calls from outside the meeting
- an over-ambitious agenda which takes too long to complete or has to be carried over to the next meeting.

The answer to all these problems is to put effort into two things:

- the objectives for the meeting
- the structure of the meeting.

Meetings often do not have real *objectives* (see page 119) so much as a list of activities. If, for example, you attend a meeting where the 'objective' is to 'discuss XY and Z' that is not really an objective at all. The objective would be whatever end result is desired from the activity of discussing XY and Z. It might be to have decided something, planned something, agreed something, or merely to have discovered people's points of view about something.

If a meeting has no objectives then it is unlikely to have an appropriate structure since the structure flows logically from the objectives. Simple advice on structure is to:

- have a logical sequence to the items on the agenda
- schedule the most important, difficult, contentious items first to catch people when they are fresh
- save a 'high note' item for the end to send people away enthusiastic
- allocate, and advertise, a time limit for each item on the agenda.

The contrast between ineffective and effective meetings can be captured under 10 headings:

Characteristics of an ineffective meeting	*Characteristics of an effective meeting*
Size over 12 participants	about 7 participants (with the proviso that they all have something useful to contribute)
Frequency of meeting Daily (because familiarity breeds contempt and leads to sloppy practices)	Preferably a maximum of once a week for the same group of participants. This makes the meeting sufficiently 'special' to keep people on their toes.
Duration over 2 hours	1 hour preferably but 2 hours should be an absolute maximum. If this isn't possible because, say, people have come from far and wide, then have proper breaks after each 1 hour period.
Objectives Either when objectives are non-existent or when they are implied and vague.	Objectives are clear, explicitly agreed and challenging.
Agenda Either when the agenda is non-existent or when it is in the chairman's head and not shared with the participants.	Either when there is a written agenda 48 hours in advance of the meeting or when the meeting starts with communal agenda setting.
Chairmanship No control, structure or summaries, ie let's people ramble on *or* hogs the whole thing, makes all the decisions	Looks after the process, ie clarifies objectives and structure. Orchestrates the discussion. Summarizes to

Characteristics of an ineffective meeting	*Characteristics of an effective meeting*
and does all the talking.	check understanding and agreement of actions.

Participation
Some people say a lot, some people say virtually nothing.

People contributing in an open, honest, enthusiastic way.

Problem solving method
problems identified but not addressed *or* people jumping to conclusions about causes/solutions and not considering the pros and cons of alternatives.

A systematic approach, ie
specifying the problem
collecting information
generating ideas
evaluating alternatives
agreeing on the best
course of action
planning implementation.

Interruptions
Messages etc are allowed to intrude into the meeting. People wander in and out to deal with things that are happening outside the meeting.

No interruptions, ie messages kept until after the meeting.

Conclusions/actions
Vague or non-existent

Specific conclusions/actions summarized and noted so that everyone knows exactly who is supposed to do what as a consequence of the meeting.

For more details that will help in running effective meetings see *Groups*, page 77, *Objectives*, page 119, *Going round in circles*, page 76, *Roles*, page 149, *Chairing meetings*, page 28.

Mistakes

We all make mistakes and whilst unwelcome they are often good for us because they jolt our complacency. Mistakes give people a shock and therefore make it more likely that they will learn.

It is commonplace to hear people claiming to learn by their mistakes but that assumes that a mistake is recognized as such. In the area of behaviour a mistake is often a hard thing to detect – particularly if you are the one who has made it! It is clearly easier to spot other people making mistakes than either to catch yourself or to admit to yourself that *you* did so. Unless you possess extraordinary powers of self-insight (see *Self-awareness* on page 153) you are likely to delude yourself into thinking that since your intentions are good your behaviour is good also. Unfortunately, the one does not necessarily follow from the other. You may *intend* to be helpful, and even think you are being helpful, by, for example, giving someone advice. The recipient of this advice may, however, find it positively unhelpful and wish that you'd shut up and listen to them.

The best way out of this quandary is to stop thinking about mistakes as such and to ask yourself regularly 'What could have gone better?' This question allows for the possibility of an actual mistake, big or small, as well as acknowledging that you can *always* do even better than you did. This acts as an excellent safeguard against complacency without the gloom and doom which tends to accompany mistakes. It is a recipe for self-improvement through a process of continuous fine tuning rather than merely being shocked into learning as a result of the occasional mistake. For more on the mechanics of *Learning from experience* see page 100 and *Reviewing* on page 147.

Motives

Motives, at their simplest, are the underlying reasons why someone is behaving in a particular way. If, for example, someone was being persistently negative in a meeting their motives might be:

- to prevent agreement being reached
- to win some concessions
- to draw attention to a particular cause
- to get their own back against someone who 'won' last time
- to draw attention to themselves

and so on.

Motives are never directly observable whereas behaviour always is. The presence of a particular motive can only be inferred by working backwards from the behaviour itself. Often people are unclear themselves about their motives for doing something so even if you question them you may not reveal the real motive.

Fortunately it is not essential to know what someone's motives are in order to deal with them effectively. It is more important to be clear about the links between the way they are behaving and the situations they are in. The reason for this is that the circumstances of the situation are just as much a cause of behaviour as the underlying motive.

For more on the mechanics of doing this see *Behaviour modification* on page 16.

Myths about behaviour

People often hold some 'odd' beliefs about behaviour. For example, it is more convenient to believe that your behaviour 'just happens' because this absolves you from having the responsibilities that accompany choice. Most of the 'myths' exposed in this section are excuses of one sort or another not to take responsibility for your own behaviour.

Here are four commonly held myths about behaviour:

1. Behaviour is born not made

This is partially true because there are some behaviours that are intact from the word go. A new-born baby can cry, suck, sneeze and is equipped with other basic reflexes, all of which are examples of observable behaviour. All the other more sophisticated behaviours develop through a process of learning and are thus more 'made' than 'born'. It is important to believe that you have acquired most of your ways of behaving because that opens up the possibility of behaviour being malleable rather than something fixed and unchanging.

2 Behaviour is caused by 'internal factors' such as motives, attitudes and feelings

Again partially true, but only half the story. The truth is that behaviour is caused simultaneously by a combination of internal *and* external factors. Usually when you wonder what makes people tick you speculate about such things as their motives, attitudes and feelings. If someone is resistant to change, for example, you might attribute this behaviour to an underlying fear of change. The fear alone does not cause the behaviour, however. It is equally true to say that the advent of the impending change has caused the behaviour in just the same way as an itch causes a scratch. So whilst internal factors are an important part of the picture the external factor of change itself triggered (ie caused) the whole sequence of events.

3 Your behaviour once formed is fixed

All your behaviour, with the exception of those reflexes that were built into the system, has been acquired over a long period of *ad hoc* learning. It follows, therefore, that there is no end to the period of acquisition. You can go on learning and adding to your repertoire of behaviours for as long as there is breath in your body. The problem is not so much whether you can or can't but rather whether you *want* to.

4 The way you behave makes very little difference

Often people maintain that it is knowing your stuff that really counts and behaviour is just the icing on the cake. Whilst it is certainly true that behaviour is no substitute for knowledge, the way you behave is the biggest single factor in making an impact on the way other people respond to you. Behaviour breeds behaviour. So far as other people are concerned, you *are* your behaviour.

The theme running through all these myths about behaviour is 'Don't blame me, it's not *my* fault.' It is obviously more convenient to blame the situation and especially *other people* for the way you react but the truth is that you, and you alone, are responsible for your behaviour. It is yours to manage and mould. For more detail on how to do this, see *Behaviour modification* on page 16.

Natural behaviour

Natural behaviour can mean one of two things. Either it refers to behaviour which does not have to be learned or it refers to behaviour which has been so thoroughly learned that it can be done 'naturally', ie without conscious thought and application.

Natural behaviours in the first sense are few and far between (see *Instincts* on page 93) since the majority of human behaviour has been acquired through an *ad hoc* learning process. The second meaning is therefore more applicable and this equates so-called natural behaviour with skilled behaviour. All natural behaviour has, therefore, become so by going through a stage of being unnatural.

People often object to practising behaviours that they do not usually use on the grounds that it isn't natural. The only way, however, to increase your repertoire of behaviours is to force yourself to use behaviours which are 'unnatural' so that with practice they reach the stage of being natural. For more on this transition see *Skilful behaviour* on page 155.

Negotiating

Negotiating is an activity that seeks to reach agreement between two or more different starting positions. Negotiation is therefore a means of getting what you want from other people and as such qualifies as a *tricky situation* (see page 168), where the way you behave is a make or break factor.

There are eight behaviours that are typical of successful negotiators and distinguish them from the less successful. (Success is defined by the extent to which the negotiator not only achieved the immediate *objective* (see page 119), but also by the extent to which the agreement stuck when implemented.) In no order of importance the eight key behaviours are:

1 Focusing on interests not positions

One of the problems frequently encountered in negotiating is that sides take up incompatible positions. Skilled negotiators don't take up positions. Instead they concentrate on the interests that lie behind the positions. A position is a decision. The interests are the reasons for the decision. Positions tend to bring things to a grinding halt. Interests are much more likely to provide footholds for finding common ground and moving ahead. For example the position might be 'I must have a promotion within six months'. The interests behind this might be:

- to have a more stimulating job
- to have extra responsibility
- to earn more money
- to qualify for a company car.

If we assume that for various reasons promotion within six months is not possible, all or some of the interests might be met in alternative ways. Agreement is more likely if both parties explore their interests rather than state their positions.

2 Exploring proposals rather than counter proposing

Less skilled negotiators are far more likely to match a proposal with a counter proposal. Unfortunately counter proposals are perceived as disagreements rather than as constructive ideas on possible courses of action. Skilled negotiators resist the temptation to counter propose and instead explore the pros and cons of each proposal as it comes up.

3 Attacking the problem not the person

Less skilled negotiators are far more likely to get locked into an attacking spiral where one side attacks the other which provokes a counter attack and so on. Skilled negotiators avoid criticizing or attacking the other person and concentrate instead on 'attacking' the problem in a no nonsense but constructive way.

4 *Sticking to the facts rather than exaggerating*

Less skilled negotiators are inclined to exaggeration. Thus they will use expressions such as 'very generous offer', 'an offer you simply can't refuse', 'mutually beneficial', to describe their own proposals. By contrast they tend to exaggerate the unacceptability of proposals from the other person, 'a derisory offer', 'completely unreasonable', 'laughable' and so on. Skilled negotiators avoid using irritators such as these and keep the emotional temperature down by sticking to the facts.

5 *Disagreeing constructively*

Disagreements are inevitable during the course of a negotiation. There is, however, a marked difference between the way negotiators disagree. Less skilled negotiators disagree in the order they think, that is, saying they disagree first and then going on to give reasons. This often provokes a negative reaction from the other person who bridles at the explicit disagreement and therefore fails to listen to the reasons – indeed, is highly likely to interrupt the reasons rather than hear them out. The skilled negotiator, by contrast, reverses the order and gives an explanation first (ie the reason for being in disagreement) and finishes by saying something like 'and that is why I disagree'. This has a more constructive effect in that the explanation becomes the focus for the other person's reaction rather than the fact of a disagreement.

6 *Being open about thoughts and feelings*

The skilled negotiator is far more likely to say things that reveal what he or she is thinking, intending and feeling than the less skilled, who reckon that to expose such things is naïve. The less skilled negotiator feels vulnerable to losing the argument and is more likely to 'keep his cards close to his chest' (see *Openness* on page 126).

7 *Asking questions*

Skilled negotiators ask at least twice as many questions as the less skilled. The less skilled are more likely to assume that they understand the other person's point of view and that the other person has the same basic information. This makes asking questions redundant. The skilled negotiator, on the other hand, asks questions not only to gain more information and understanding but also as an alternative to disagreeing bluntly and as a means of putting forward suggestions (ie possible courses of action said as questions. See *Idea-having* on page 86).

8 Summarizing

The skilled negotiator *summarizes* (see page 159) and tests understanding far more frequently than the less skilled. The less skilled negotiator prefers to leave things vague and ambiguous fearing that explicitness will jeopardize any agreement. The skilled negotiator knows that explicitness aids common understanding and leads to a quality agreement that is more likely to stick.

Non-verbal behaviour

Non-verbal or visual behaviour covers a wide range of different aspects including:

- facial expressions
- eyes
- hand movements
- gestures with hands and arms
- leg movements
- body posture
- spatial distance and orientation.

In addition, there are some fringe areas such as clothes, physique and general appearance.

There is overwhelming evidence from many research studies to show that visual behaviours play a larger part in communications between people than is usually supposed.

It seems that, without necessarily being able to describe how they do it, people make judgements and form impressions based on the visual behaviours they see other people using. Perhaps the most dramatic example of this is when people meet for the first time. Within seconds visual behaviours are sending signals which create a favourable or an unfavourable impression. Initial judgements are formed about whether the other person is friendly or unfriendly, confident or timid, trustworthy or untrustworthy, nice or nasty. Sometimes these first impressions are so strong that they stubbornly linger and defy revision even when different signals are being transmitted by subsequent visual behaviours.

Clearly the great advantage of thinking about your visual as well as your verbal behaviour is that you can choose visual behaviours which help rather than hinder progress towards your objective. You may be in the habit of using some visual behaviours that run the risk of giving the other person a poor impression of you. The secret of success is to concentrate on some simple combinations. If you do just one thing in isolation it probably will not have the desired effect because people gain a general, overall impression from a combination of:

- your facial expression and head movements
- gestures with your hands and arms
- the rest of your body including your legs.

All three aspects need to be practised so that they all come together to give the right impression.

Here are some combinations of visual behaviours. Practise doing less of the left hand ones and more of the right hand ones.

People will tend to see you as DEFENSIVE if you:	If you want to come across as FRIENDLY and CO-OPERATIVE adopt the following combinations:
Face and head	*Face and head*
Don't look at the other person. Avoid eye contact or immediately look away when it happens.	Look at the other person's face. Smile. Nod your head as the other person is talking.
Hands and arms	*Hands and arms*
Clench your hands. Cross your arms. Constantly rub an eye, nose or ear.	Have open hands. Uncrossed arms. Hands to face occasionally.

Body
Cross your legs.
Lean away from the other person.
Swivel your feet towards the door.

Body
Uncrossed legs.
Lean forward slightly.
Move close to the other person.

People will tend to see you as
ANXIOUS if you:

If you want to appear
CONFIDENT adopt the following
combinations:

Face and head
Blink your eyes frequently.
Lick your lips.
Keep clearing your throat.

Face and head
Don't blink your eyes.
Look into the other person's
eyes.
Thrust your chin forward.

Hands and arms
Open and close your hands
frequently.
Put your hand over your mouth
while speaking.
Tug at an ear.

Hands and arms
Keep hands away from your
face.
'Steeple' your finger tips
together.
If standing, have hands
together behind you in an
'at ease' position.

Body
Fidget in your chair.
Jig your feet up and down.

Body
Stay still, no sudden
movements, no wriggling.
If seated, lean back with legs
out in front of you.
If standing, keep straight.

People will tend to see you as
OVERBEARING and AGGRESSIVE if
you:

If you want to appear
THOUGHTFUL try the following
combinations:

Face and head
Stare at the other person.
Have a wry 'I've heard it all
before' type of smile.
Raise your eyebrows in
amazement or disbelief.
Look over the top of spectacles.

Face and head
When listening, look at the
the other person for about
three quarters of the time.
Tilt your head to one side
slightly.

Hands and arms
Point your finger at the other person.
Thump your fist on the table.
Rub the back of your neck.

Hands and arms
Slowly stroke your chin or the bridge of your nose.
If you wear spectacles, take them off and put an earframe in your mouth.

Body
Stand while the other person remains seated.
Stride around.
If seated, lean right back with both hands behind your head and legs splayed out in front of you.

Body
Lean forward to speak.
Lean back to listen.
Keep your legs still (no jiggling).

Non-verbal behaviours need to accompany and reinforce what you are saying, your verbal behaviour. It is the combination of verbal and non-verbal that is likely to have the desired effect. For guidance on *verbal behaviours* see page 170.

Objectives

Objectives are important because they act as an essential backcloth to behaviour itself. Behaviour in a vacuum may be very interesting but that's about all. Decisions about the effectiveness and appropriateness of different behaviours can only be made within the context of particular situations and specific objectives.

Despite this, resistance to the objective setting message is high. Typical blockages to objective setting include the following:

- People are often not clear about what an objective actually is. They get confused about the differences between *activities* and objectives, about short term and long term objectives and about semantics.
- People often prefer the excitement of 'playing things by ear' or having a very vague open-ended objective to the discipline of pinpointing a precise objective.
- People often prefer to rationalize *after* the event and convince

themselves things went well and 'according to plan', rather than compare what was actually achieved against the objective.

- People often feel that pinpointing a precise objective wastes time that could be used more productively getting on with the job in hand.
- People have often had bad experiences with objective setting. For example, they may have been encouraged to stick their necks out and set an objective and then been clobbered for not achieving it. Alternatively, they may have found objective setting a dull ritual that didn't make any difference to anything.
- People often feel safer if they play things close to their chests and don't reveal their hand too early. Since they wouldn't want to declare their real objective, even if they had one, they see little point in having one at all.
- People find that, by and large, they get by without bothering about objectives. They think they've been successful if they have kept busy. Never mind if they were busy doing all the wrong things!

An objective is a clear, precise forecast of what you want to achieve some time in the future. The objective could forecast achievement in the immediate future (like thirty minutes, one hour, two hours, etc), in the short term (like today, this week, this month), in the longer term (like this quarter, this half year, this year) or in the distant future (like two years, three years, four years, five years, a decade, a lifetime).

Irrespective of these differences in time, a respectable objective has certain known qualities as follows:

- Any objective has two parts to it:

    A forecast of the *end result*
    Indicators of success.

- Any objective should be in step with the circumstances of the situation as you know or understand them.
- Any objective should be realistic or, in other words, possible to achieve successfully within the forecasted time span.
- Any objective should be challenging or, in other words, pitched at a level of achievement where you are going to have to strive to pull it off (and have deserved feelings of satisfaction if you succeed).

It is important to have clear, precise objectives when interacting. Here are some of the benefits:

- The objective helps you to be clear about what you have to *do* in a bid to get it to come true.
- The objective makes it easy to compare the actual outcome with your prediction. This means you can be quite certain about total success, relative success and failure and, therefore, be in a better position to learn from experience.
- The objective helps you to organize your behaviour. It means that you can spot irrelevancies and be better at controlling your behaviour so that it contributes to the achievement of your objective.
- The objective helps you to communicate to others what you want to achieve. Doing this helps them to decide whether they can subscribe to it or not.

Objective setting is a skill which, like any other, develops with practice. Here is a step by step routine to follow when setting an objective for an interaction:

1 Clarify the overall aim (ie the longer term end result).
2 In the light of the overall aim, set an immediate end result by answering the question 'What result do I want to achieve by the end of this interaction?'
3 Work out indicators of success by answering the question 'How shall I know that the end result has been successfully achieved?'

Here is an example of an objective set this way.

OVERALL AIM
The customer has bought goods to the value of X by the year end.

END RESULT
By the end of the meeting I will have established rapport with the customer.

INDICATORS OF SUCCESS
The customer has asked at least six questions about me/my work.
The customer has 'opened up' to me about a significant current problem.

The customer has relaxed sufficiently to volunteer at least a couple
of personal details (about outside interests, family, etc).

We have booked a date, time and place for our next meeting.

The customer has specifically asked me to provide some additional
data for our next meeting.

All achieved within an hour (longer than the customer originally
scheduled, ie he was 'happy' to overrun).

Finally, here is a check list to help you determine whether an
objective is satisfactory:

1 Has the objective got an end result together with some indicators
of success?
2 Does the objective pinpoint an end result, as opposed to merely
describing an activity? (An activity is something you do. An end
result is what is achieved as a result of doing it.)
3 Is the objective achievable by the end of the interaction?
4 Are the indicators of success obviously linked with the end result?
(Sometimes people drift off and dream up indicators which don't
adequately tie in with the end result.)
5 Are the indicators of success precise enough to enable the
achievement to be assessed with considerable certainty?
6 Do the indicators of success cover
    quantity
    quality
    reactions (behaviour)
    and time?

Observing behaviour

Observing behaviour is easy because behaviour, verbal and non-
verbal, is always overt and therefore eminently observable. The
difficulty is not in the observing but in the interpreting of what has
been observed. For example, suppose you observed someone in a
meeting intermittently tapping their left foot. This would be easy
enough to notice but not so easy to interpret. It might signify a
whole host of different things, such as the person is:

• impatient to finish the meeting

- irritated with whatever the speaker is saying
- limbering up to put a point themselves
- physically uncomfortable.

Or, of course, it might simply be a habit the person has acquired that has no particular significance.

It is important to observe behaviour as accurately as possible because the more accurate the observation the more this helps you to place a valid interpretation on what you have seen or heard. Even accurate observation will not *guarantee* that you will reach the right conclusion but it certainly makes it much more likely.

Observing behaviour is greatly aided by having a system of some kind to follow. The system acts as a discipline to ensure that you concentrate sufficiently on observation instead of being tempted to jump to conclusions. There are basically two different systems on offer. One is the 'clean sheet approach', where you make copious notes on *everything* to do with a person's behaviour. Typically this involves writing down lots of verbatim quotes and also making notes on any non-verbal goings-on. Afterwards the notes are scanned to identify themes and patterns and to interpret them. An alternative system is the 'checklist approach', where you decide in advance which verbal and/or non-verbal behaviours you are going to observe and devise a number of categories to monitor behaviour against. This has the obvious advantage of reducing the sheer volume of data to be gathered and processed but the disadvantage of being inflexible and possibly missing significant happenings because the category system didn't allow for them.

The answer is to use the 'clean sheet approach' when scrutinizing one or two people's behaviour and the checklist approach for observing behaviour in groups and meetings.

For more information on categories see *Categories of behaviour* on page 26).

OKness

OKness is a concept (American as you might guess!) from *transactional analysis* (see page 167). In transactional analysis (TA) it is assumed that our *habitual* ways of feeling and behaving largely stem from the way we feel about ourselves in relation to other people.

The conclusions we characteristically reach about this were learned in childhood when we needed to make sense of the many confusing and contradictory recordings in our three ego-states. These assumptions about ourselves in relation to others are called life positions because they tend to dictate the positions we take up throughout life.

The life positions can be generalized into 'I'm OK' or 'I'm not OK', and 'You're OK' or 'You're not OK'. They fit together to form four basic life positions:

You're OK with me

Withdrawal	*OKness*
A common position for people who feel inadequate when they compare themselves to others. People in this position feel low or depressed and spend much energy avoiding people.	A potentially healthy position from the Adult ego-state, reached after a large number of OK experiences with others. It concludes: 'You and I are important. Together we can solve problems constructively.'

I'm not _____ *I'm OK*
OK with me _____ *with me*

Futility	*Arrogance*
This is a despairing life position. People in it lose interest in living, they become apathetic about their lot and get nowhere with other people or their own lives. (In extreme cases this leads to madness and/or suicide/homicide.)	The position of people when they feel victimized or persecuted. They blame others for their miseries. It is a distrustful life position and much energy is spent getting rid of people. (Extreme examples are delinquents and criminals with persecution complexes.)

You're not OK with me

Even though people may have favourite life positions and spend a majority of their time in one or other of the corners, everyone experiences all four at different times and in different situations. In particular, it is common for people to oscillate between withdrawal and arrogance. In many people's experience futility and OKness are rarer positions. OKness is the only position that requires an Adult ego-state (see page 57).

Life-positions throw light on why it is that some people tend to be winners and some losers in life. There is not much you can do to make radical changes to other people's basic life positions, but you can use your awareness of the four 'OK – Not OK' positions to understand why you sometimes feel hopeless, depressed, victimized and so on. Self-understanding is not in itself going to bring about changes, but it can be half the battle in recognizing what is happening early enough and encouraging you to do something about it.

What is it like being in the 'I'm, OK – You're OK' position? There are two aspects to it; things to do with yourself (that's the I'm OK bit) and things to do with the other person (that's the You're OK bit).

I'm OK with me

You feel confident, within your depth, alert and interested in what's going on. You feel sure you are in touch with the salient aspects of the situation and that you have an important contribution to make. You don't feel the need to prove yourself, to seek approval, to be careful what you say, or to put up a façade of any kind. You don't feel compelled to say a great deal, to be interesting, to be the life and soul of the occasion. You are free of feelings of guilt, worry, anxiety, embarrassment, envy or jealousy. You do not feel competitive so much as creative and co-operative. You are happy to react 'there and then' even if this means expressing half-baked ideas. You do not feel inhibited because you haven't prepared adequately or fear that other people might catch you out or ridicule you.

You're OK with me

You accept that the other person is important – just as important as you, no better, no worse. This means that you seek their views, listen to their opinions and actively consider their contributions. You do not try to catch them out, to trap them or to expose them as inadequate in any way. On the other hand you don't wrap things up in cotton wool. You don't worry about offending them (OK people don't get offended). You praise and criticize as appropriate but always authentically rather than to create an effect. You are glad about their successes and triumphs. You are realistic about their faults and weaknesses. Just because they are OK with you it doesn't mean you are blind to their inadequacies or view them through rose-coloured spectacles. They are OK with you, warts and all! You have confidence that they will respond to your OKness and that together you can tackle whatever has to be accomplished in coherent partnership.

Since we all experience all four life-positions at different times and in different situations we can at least increase the frequency of OKness. Two practical tips for increasing the probability of OKness in your relationships with others are:

- Work out what sort of situations seem to cause you to experience the four different feelings. If you can identify some of them, you may find you can arrange things so that you avoid some of the situations that make you feel Not-OK and increase your exposure to situations where you experience OKness.
- In situations where you don't feel OK you can use your Adult to prevent the feelings 'surfacing' in your overt behaviour and to control your behaviour so that it is conducted on an I'm OK – You're OK basis. This will not necessarily stop the Not-OK feelings but it at least contains them so that they don't damage the transaction. Often behaving OK and getting the resultant strokes, loops back and causes you actually to feel OK.

If, through self-awareness and conscious effort, you can get more frequently into an I'm OK – You're OK position, you are, in effect, inviting other people to adopt an I'm OK – You're OK stance also. Since behaviour breeds behaviour these are mutually reinforcing positions and lead to increased trust and the release of energies in more productive and enjoyable ways.

Openness

Openness is a value that tends to pervade all the behavioural sciences. This is not only for ethical considerations but more pragmatically because there is an assumption that if you treat others as you would wish to be treated, they will respond in kind. In other words, if you are open with people they will tend to reciprocate by being more open themselves.

Being open and honest about what you are thinking, how you are feeling and why you are doing whatever you are doing is deemed to be efficient and helpful because otherwise people waste precious time and energy trying to 'second guess' what you are up to. No-one has access to your thoughts, feelings and motives, only to your actions (ie behaviour), and so unless you are open in revealing them, people are obliged to indulge in speculation.

Openness features particularly strongly in *Assertiveness* (see page 8) and in *Transactional analysis* (see page 167).

Personality

Personality is an all-embracing term that covers everything about you; your outward behaviour as well as all the underlying factors, such as *beliefs* (see page 21), *attitudes* (see page 12) and *feelings* (see page 66).

People often assume that personality and behaviour are one and the same and this leads to the erroneous assumption that because the fundamentals of your personality are relatively fixed so also is your behaviour. The difference between personality and behaviour becomes clearer if you think of your personality as the thread of consistency that runs through everything you do. Your personality sets boundaries on what you can and cannot do in rather the same way that your physical build also sets constraints. Suppose, for example, you have a so-called extraverted personality, this means that for most of the time in most situations you will tend to think, feel and behave in outward going ways. But even a dyed-in-the-wool extravert will sometimes choose to behave more demurely. This doesn't mean they have changed their personality, it merely demonstrates that even extraverts are capable of modifying their behaviour.

Even more frequently there are people who claim to be introverted, (in other words they think and feel as an introvert) but who nonetheless over-compensate and behave in extraverted ways. So your personality sets very broad limits, but whatever its nature it leaves you with plenty of room to manoeuvre when it comes to ways of behaving.

People often use their personalities as an excuse not to bother to take responsibility for their own behaviour. 'You must take me as you find me', 'A leopard can't change his spots' and other maxims take an essentially pessimistic view about the malleability of behaviour. All the evidence suggests, however, that whilst our basic personalities are relatively unchanging (except in response to fairly drastic interventions such as the use of drugs, brainwashing and brain damage as a result of an accident or stroke) our overt behaviour is amenable to a process of continual modification and change. (For more advice on how to do this see *Behaviour modification* on page 16.)

Persuasiveness

All of us, whatever our walk of life, are frequently in situations where we want to persuade someone or, in other words, influence someone to do what we want them to do (eg a salesperson trying to persuade a buyer or a negotiator trying to persuade another negotiator). You may not consider yourself as either a salesperson or a negotiator but you are a persuader nonetheless. Think how often you have an idea that you need to 'sell' to your boss or to colleagues. Think how often, say in a meeting or discussion, you have a point of view that you want to persuade other people to agree with or adopt. The plain fact is that in most of your interactions with other people you are seeking to exert some influence – to persuade.

Success depends on three interrelated factors:

1 The starting position of the people you wish to influence

They are likely to be somewhere on the following continuum

1	2	3	4	5
↑	↑	↑	↑	↑
Diametric-ally opposed to your point of view	More against than for, with some major objections	Neutral, neither for nor against, your point of view	More for than against, but with some reservations	In total agreement with your point of view

Clearly the five positions along this continuum are an over-simplification and there are various shades of grey in between each position. It is obvious that the starting position affects what it is realistic to aim for. Thus, for example, persuading someone from position 1 and expecting to convert them to position 5 is unrealistic. Generally speaking it is best to aim to move someone two places to the right:

From 1 to 3
From 2 to 4
From 3 to 5.

4 to 5 is relatively easy and if someone starts off at 5 they don't need any persuading at all (attempts to persuade them may irritate them so much that they start to move to the left!).

2 What you say

Clearly the subject matter of the persuasion is going to influence the outcome. If it is inappropriate or if you are underprepared then the likelihood of success is reduced.

The sequence of what you say makes a considerable difference to success. Persuasiveness is enhanced if your message unfolds in a chronological sequence, ie:

- an initial benefit statement to catch the interest of the other person
- your idea

- the potential benefits of the idea for the person
- the evidence/rationale to back up the benefits you are claiming
- the diffusion of possible objections before they are raised
- a summary of the idea and its main benefits.

This sequence is designed to synchronize with the unspoken questions that the other person is likely to be formulating:

- Why should I listen to this?
- What is this about?
- What's in it for me?
- Can I believe this?
- Yes, but . . . ?
- Have I got this right?

Different circumstances and the type of situation will make some of these aspects more or less important. For example, if it is an informal discussion with just one person, you may 'relax' the formal sequence set out above. If, on the other hand, you are seeking to influence a group of people in a more formal meeting, then consciously working through each stage in the sequence is more appropriate.

3 How you behave

Your behaviour is at least as important as the content of what you have to say. If your behaviour is inappropriate it will detract from, even negate, the message and seriously reduce the likelihood of success. These are the key persuasive behaviours:

- a strong, enthusiastic voice
- fluent speaking without hesitations and urrs and umms
- the use of open-ended questions (ie that avoid yes/no answers) that begin with what, when, where, how and who
- the use of silences and pauses rather than fillers and 'non-words' such as 'OK', 'Right', 'You know'
- looking at the other person for at least half the time and holding eye contact for a complete thought (usually about five seconds)
- using gestures with hands and arms to add emphasis to points. (Gestures are more convincing when unplanned and spontaneous.) After a gesture your hands and arms should always return to an 'at rest' position.

So, in summary, your persuasiveness depends on two equally important aspects:

- what you say (content)
- how you say it (behaviour)

Planning behaviour

Planning is acknowledged as necessary for most activities in life but strangely there is often a blind spot when it comes to planning *behaviour*. There are a number of reasons for this:

- People think of behaviour as a vast amorphous thing which is impossible to plan.
- People believe that behaviour is best left to natural, spontaneous expression.
- People prefer to be opportunists and leave themselves the flexibility of 'seeing what happens and reacting accordingly'.
- People argue that if you don't know the people you are going to meet you can't plan how best to behave.

None of these reasons provides an adequate excuse for leaving an important ingredient like behaviour to chance.

Behaviour is just as amenable to a planning process as, say, constructing a building. It only requires behaviour to be broken down into some specifics, the equivalent of building blocks, and for those specifics to be cast into a coherent plan of action.

Behaviour categories (see page 26) are the key to breaking behaviour down into manageable proportions. However, before deciding which categories to employ, it is necessary to have:

- a clear idea of the objective you wish to achieve
- some notion of what behaviour you *ideally* want from the other person, or persons, in order to achieve your objective.

Once you have these you are then in a position to work out which behaviours to use and which behaviours to avoid yourself in order to shape the reactions you want from the other person. The mechanics of putting together a behaviour plan will become clear if you look at two other sections: *Verbal behaviour* on page 170 and *Non-verbal behaviour* on page 116.

The following is an example of a behaviour plan arrived at using the behaviour category approach.

The situation

Imagine that you are a manager with three supervisors reporting to you. One of them, Bill, was promoted to a supervisory position a few months ago. Technically he is excellent but you have noticed that he is falling down on the supervisory aspects of his job. For example, he tends to pitch in and sort things out for himself and does not spend enough time on man-management. You decide to help Bill improve his performance as a supervisor.

The overall aim

To have improved Bill's performance as a supervisor.

The immediate objective

End Result: To have agreed criteria for judging Bill's performance as a supervisor.

Indicators of success

- We will have produced at least six criteria.
- Each criterion will be specific enough for Bill and me to judge performance against it without hesitation and to reach the same conclusion.
- Each criterion will be concerned with the supervisory aspects of Bill's job and not the technical aspects.
- Bill will have spontaneously suggested at least half the criteria himself.
- Bill remarks that the criteria have helped him to be clearer about what is involved in being a good supervisor.
- Bill volunteers the suggestion that we should meet to review his performance against the criteria quite soon.
- All to be achieved within one and a half hours.

The behaviours I want from Bill

proposing and suggesting
supporting and building

The behaviours I don't want from Bill

disagreeing and difficulty stating
explaining

The behaviours I will use to get what I want from Bill

seeking ideas
suggesting and building
supporting

The behaviours I will avoid

proposing
disagreeing
seeking clarification

This plan makes it as likely as possible that I shall employ behaviours that are appropriate in two vital ways:

1 to achieve the immediate objective and thus have taken a significant step towards achieving the overall aim
2 to shape Bill's behaviour so that he is positive and helpful.

A plan can do nothing more. It is then up to me to implement it successfully by controlling my behaviour whilst keeping an eye on progress towards the indicators of success. In this way behaviour is eminently plannable. The existence of my plan does not mean, however, that I shall stick rigidly to it come what may. I might have to modify it in the light of circumstances. Suppose, for example, Bill is very forthcoming and has lots of ideas on possible criteria. My plan assumed that I would have to work for these by actively seeking ideas. If in the event there were plenty of ideas then my plan to seek them would become redundant. Neither objectives nor plans are an invitation to become inflexible. They need to be constantly revised, up or down, depending on actual circumstances rather than assumed circumstances (see *Assumptions* on page 12).

Positive reinforcement

People do things (ie behave) in anticipation of certain consequences. If, after having done something, the consequence is 'nice' then the behaviour is said to have been positively reinforced.

Positive reinforcement encourages people and its opposite, punishment, discourages people (see *Punishment* on page 142.) Most people find life a mixture of nice and nasty experiences and behaviour is aimed at maximizing the nice experiences and minimizing the nasty ones. This sounds very bland but in practice it is complicated by the fact that what is nice for one person is nasty for another and *vice versa*. For example, one person may find it nice to be rewarded for good work by being taken out to a slap-up dinner and another person may be embarrassed by the whole business and have preferred a quiet word of thanks. A third person may resent the waste of money and prefer to have been given a bonus to spend as he wishes.

Reinforcement, or lack of it, plays a major part in all behaviour and is especially important when attempting to get people to do what you want them to do. Here is a simple illustration. Suppose your boss asks you for suggestions about how a particular problem could be solved and you immediately respond with some ideas. If your boss listens, agrees with your suggestions and even adds to them, providing you found this 'nice', your behaviour of putting forward ideas has been positively reinforced. In similar circumstances you are, therefore, more likely to come forward with ideas again.

If, on the other hand, your boss kept chasing you for ideas and generally putting the pressure on you until he got ideas that he considered satisfactory, then, providing you found the pressure 'nasty' and its cessation 'nice', behaviour of putting forward ideas would also have been reinforced. This, however, would not be positive so much as negative reinforcement, ie it was nice when the pressure stopped. Your boss's behaviour of chasing you and putting pressure on is likely to have been positively reinforced, ie it was 'nice' for him when you finally came up with ideas which he found satisfactory. So, at the same time, your behaviour is being negatively reinforced and your boss's behaviour positively reinforced.

So positive reinforcement is anything that happens soon after the behaviour in question that is welcomed by the recipient. Negative reinforcement is something unwelcome that happens before or during the behaviour in question has occurred. Both types of reinforcement *increase* the frequency of behaviour.

Whenever you want to get someone to do more of something be careful to use either or both of the types of reinforcement. Positive reinforcement is the most straightforward. For more on this see *Behaviour modification* on page 16.

Praise

Praising people, if it is done authentically, is a behaviour which is generally welcome and tends to encourage people to do well. Indeed most people, however accomplished and apparently confident, suffer from praise deprivation. It is a common experience that when things go well nothing gets said but when things go badly it is certainly noticed and *all hell breaks out*.

How can you praise people authentically so that it functions as an encourager? Here is a table contrasting effective with less effective forms of praising.

Ineffective praise	*Effective praise*
1 Generalized praise – such as 'You're doing a good job Charlie.' This is meaningless and it generally rolls off the back of the person without effect.	1 Specific praise – such as 'Charlie you did a great job handling that unpleasant customer with a complaint this afternoon.' This communicates to the person what you observed or heard that deserves praise.
2 Praise with no further explanation as to *why* a behaviour is being commended. This 'discounts' the person being praised by assuming they will respond with higher productivity and better morale	2 Continuing with 'The reason I think it was such a good job is because you appeared interested, asked questions, wrote down the facts, asked the customer what she thought we should

Ineffective praise	*Effective praise*
merely as a parrot-like response.	do to make it right.' Praise of this kind demonstrates that you really mean it and in addition renders useful feedback that the person stands to learn from.
3 Praise for expected performance. This may be questioned, eg if Sue, who always gets in on time, is greeted one morning with 'Sue, you are on time today! Well done!' She may well be puzzled.	3 Praise for better than expected results . . . for exceeding the target, for making an extra effort, for being on time when usually late and so on.
4 The 'sandwich' system – praise is given first to make the person receptive to criticism (the real reason for the transaction), which is then followed by another piece of praise, hoping thereby to encourage the person to 'try harder' next time and feel better about the criticism.	4 Praise, when deserved, given by itself is believable, when mixed with criticism it is suspect. Authentic relations develop better when people talk 'straight'. When praise is in order, give it, when criticism is deserved, give it. Don't mix the two.
5 Praise perceived by the person as a 'carrot' mainly to encourage them to work harder in the future.	5 Praise that is geared to the here and now and does not seek to put a mortgage on the future.
6 Praise handed out lavishly only when more senior people are present. People soon realize that the real purpose is to impress superiors rather than to give authentic praise.	6 Praise given when it is deserved, not just on special occasions to give a good impression to a third party.

Presenting

Giving a presentation is a classic example of where your behaviour is at least as important as the content of what you have to say. If the behaviour is inappropriate it will detract from, or even destroy, the message the presentation is designed to convey.

The key behaviours that help a presentation to be effective are:

1 Eye contact on one person at a time for a complete thought, usually for about five seconds.
2 Strong vocal projection conveying confidence and enthusiasm. Speak as if there were twice as many people in the audience than there actually are.
3 Use silences and pauses rather than fillers and non-words.
4 Stationary feet and hips so that energy is released upwards into appropriate gestures. Pretend your feet have been cemented to the floor.
5 Hands and arms relaxed at your sides except when making gestures to add emphasis to a point. Gestures are more convincing when unplanned and spontaneous. After a gesture your hands and arms should always fall back to your sides.
6 Pitch and pace should be varied to avoid monotone and an uninteresting delivery.
7 Use simple visual aids (preferably diagrams and pictures rather than words) to enhance the main messages. Remember that 75 per cent of all we know has come from seeing.

All these behavioural skills fall into the easier said than done category but they are all learnable techniques that can be mastered with practice.

So far as the contents of the presentation are concerned, persuasiveness is enhanced if the message unfolds in a chronological sequence as follows:

1 The initial benefit statement. This is a short statement designed to catch the interest of the listeners.
2 The idea.

3 The advantages, ie the direct and indirect results of implementing the idea.

4 The evidence, ie the rationale that proves that the advantages will come from the idea.

5 The objections. This deals with possible objections listeners may be formulating about the idea before they have a chance to raise them. Dealing with them in an honest, open way diffuses the objections.

6 The summary. A quick recap of the idea and its main advantages.

7 Any questions?

For more on *persuasiveness* see page 128.

Preventing unwanted feelings

Feelings, as we saw in the entry under that heading (see pages 66 to 69), either help or hinder your behaviour. Unwanted feelings are those that hinder your behaviour such that you are not functioning at the level you are capable of. Feelings such as anger, worry and guilt are only worth having if they provoke you into doing something effective. Unfortunately, such feelings often tend to be both unpleasant to experience *and* to hinder behaviour. You are hindered when:

● you can't talk candidly with someone even though you want to
● you can't settle down to work on a project even though it interests you
● you are restless and broody
● you don't join in some enjoyable activity because of a gnawing feeling that you ought to be working
● you can't introduce yourself to someone who appeals to you
● your anger keeps you from thinking clearly
● you can't sleep because something is bothering you
● you can't say what you want to say because you are so nervous and so on!

The problems with unwanted feelings are that they tend to hinder us in the here and now even though the feelings are often associated with past or future events. Worry and guilt are excellent examples of this. You worry in the here and now about things in the future which may never happen. You feel guilty in the here and now about things that happened in the past which you cannot correct. In both cases the present moment is being spoilt by fretting needlessly over past or future moments.

What, then, can be done to prevent (*not* suppress but actually *prevent*) unproductive, unwanted feelings? It is important to be realistic. The objective is to prevent, or at least nip in the bud, unwanted feelings. In other words, the aim is to neutralize a troublesome feeling rather than to replace it with a positive feeling. If you were prone to feeling miserable, for example, the aim is to prevent feelings of misery rather than to swop them for feelings of ecstasy.

There are really two options when it comes to preventing unwanted feelings and the following diagram showing the chronological sequence of events helps to pinpoint them:

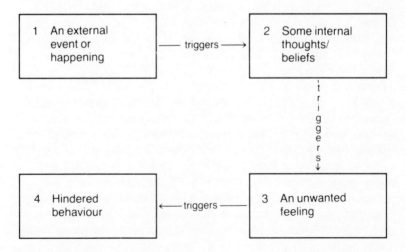

Option 1: Avoid the external events

Since the whole sequence of events begins with an external event, one option is to identify what external events tend to trigger unproductive feelings and to arrange to avoid or change the external events themselves. The snag with this is that it is often impossible to avoid the triggering events altogether and in any case it might be better to face them squarely and control your reactions to the events rather than the events themselves. However, even if you draw a blank, it is always worth checking to see whether or not you can influence the external event that starts the sequence, so either while you are being hindered by an unproductive feeling or after an experience where you were hindered ask yourself: 'What external event has triggered this feeling?'

If you can identify it, ask yourself 'Can I do anything to avoid or minimize my exposure to this external event in the future?'

If the answer is yes, firm up an appropriate avoidance plan. If the answer is no, avoidance isn't viable in this case and you will need the second strategy as follows:

Option 2: Replace the thoughts and beliefs

Intervene between the thoughts/beliefs and their attendant feelings. The idea here is consciously to replace the thoughts that trigger an unproductive feeling with other ones that do not. Since a feeling is always heralded by a thought, and since we have the ability to control our thoughts, then thinking offers the best hope for the prevention of unproductive feelings. The snag with this option is that it requires people to be rational and let their 'heads rule their hearts'. This sort of control is harder for emotional people to practise and yet they are the ones who need it most! Emotional people often reject this option as unhealthy, unnatural and unethical.

As we saw under *Beliefs* (see page 21) it is easy to fall prey to some recurring unrealistic thoughts or beliefs which cause you to feel upset whenever they are violated so, either while you are being hindered by an unproductive feeling or after an experience where you were hindered, or when you feel vulnerable to the onset of an unproductive feeling, ask yourself: 'How can I make more effective use of this present moment?'

Force yourself to *think* of an effective here-and-now action and go ahead and do it.

Other ways of thinking are available to jerk you free from the clutches of an unproductive feeling. They are all conscious thoughts and once you have experimented with them you'll be able to adopt your favourites or replace them with your own. Examples are:

- No-one can make me *feel* unproductive.
- I, and I alone, am in charge of my feelings.
- I will decide how to feel about that.
- I am OK.
- I can do it.
- It's OK to . . .
- Why should I choose to feel upset?
- Why should I let *him/her* decide how I am going to feel?

There are other sections in this book that focus in more detail on various unwanted feelings. You can take your pick from the following: *Anger*, page 4, *Boredom*, page 23, *Depression*, page 49, *Feeling hurt*, page 64, *Guilt*, page 80, *Inadequacy*, page 88, *Inhibition*, page 90, *Jealousy*, page 97, *Worry*, page 175.

Process

Process is the word used to describe *how* someone or a group is tackling a task. This is in contrast to *what* the person or group is tackling, ie the task itself.

The task might be to review the progress of a project or to plan a piece of action or to analyse a problem or to decide on the best solution to a problem. Examples of process (ie hows) might be agreeing a common understanding of the objective, deciding in which order to do things, apportioning time, deciding how best to organize a group. Processes are therefore means, whereas the task itself is an end. Achieving the task is top priority but process is vital because it either helps or hinders the achievement of the task.

People are often process 'blind', seeing only tasks and under-estimating the importance of process aspects. Awareness of process tends to dawn on people in a chronological sequence which typically goes like this:

1 *Structural awareness*, ie having clear objectives, a plan and a time schedule.
2 *Role awareness*, ie having a co-ordinator, leader or chairperson.
3 *Behavioural awareness*, ie using behaviours that are appropriate to the circumstances of the occasion.
4 *Emotional awareness*, ie being open about feelings and having empathy for how other people are feeling

Of course, some people fail to comprehend all four process aspects. They may chug along believing that structure is all there is to it or that a combination of structure and roles is the answer. Whilst it is certainly true that *any* process is better than none, awareness of all four aspects best equips people to deal with all eventualities.

For further information on process issues see *Groups* on page 77 and *Teams* on page 161.

Punishment

Punishment is the opposite of *positive reinforcement* (see page 134) and it decreases behaviour. If, for example, your boss asked you for ideas but each time you produced one he totally disagreed with it and rejected it out of hand then, assuming you found this unpleasant, your behaviour of putting forward ideas has been punished. This would make you less likely to behave like this in similar circumstances in the future.

If you tend to be a 'hard-liner', you will be attracted to punishment as a way of controlling people's behaviour. Be warned, however, that punishment has two major disadvantages.

First, evidence shows that punishment only temporarily suppresses behaviour rather than permanently changing it. As many exasperated parents and teachers have discovered, when the punishment, or the threat of it, ceases, the old behaviour tends to pop up again! The only way to ensure that the unwanted behaviour does not reappear is to keep it dampened down by more punishments. So punishment tends to lead to more punishment.

To illustrate the fact that punishment only temporarily suppresses behaviour, consider the following incident. Imagine you have an office with large windows looking out over an open-plan office; through these windows you can see what your subordinates are up to. You notice time and time again that one of them keeps reading a newspaper instead of working. Knowing that this particular subordinate is sensitive to criticism, you decide to reprimand him in the open-plan office where many of his colleagues at neighbouring desks will hear what is going on. After you have done this, you are pleased to notice that he does not read the newspaper again.

From your point of view, the punishment exactly fitted the crime and has been totally effective in stopping the unwanted behaviour. This successful experience makes it more likely that you will use public reprimands again in similar circumstances in the future and, naturally, you conclude that public reprimands work!

But do they? Certainly it appears so, since you did not see the subordinate reading his newspaper again. However, if it were possible to keep careful watch over a longer period, you would discover two interesting things. Firstly, whenever you were absent from your office, the subordinate would very probably read his newspaper – in effect, the subordinate has merely learned not to read his newspaper when you are around! This is obviously not the rip-roaring success you imagined it was. Secondly, in the absence of further punishments, the subordinate would gradually slip into reading his newspaper again, even when you were around.

The second disadvantage of punishment is that rather like potent drugs, it leads to unwanted side-effects. It is very likely that the subordinate you publicly rebuked for reading his newspaper will:

- use every opportunity to tell everyone what a swine you are
- waste time and energy plotting how to get his revenge
- engage in minor, or even major, acts of sabotage that will inconvenience you.

Presumably, none of these reactions would be welcome by you; the punishment that appeared so successful at first sight has backfired.

The answer is to use punishment sparingly, very much as a last resort. Another useful way to use punishment is in combination with positive reinforcement. This is the 'carrot and the stick' approach, the carrot being positive reinforcement and the stick punishment. Even then it is best to err on the side of too much reinforcement rather than too much punishment.

Rapport

Establishing rapport is the process of getting on the right wavelength with someone – usually, but not inevitably, with someone you are meeting for the first time. Once established, rapport makes it more likely that there will be genuine understanding and agreement and that the interaction will be mutually beneficial and enjoyable.

The actual mechanics of establishing rapport have been investigated very carefully and there is no doubt that it is a behavioural phenomenon. When you meet somebody, especially if it is the first time of meeting, your senses are working flat out to process all the data. You can see what they look like. You can feel the handshake, you can hear what they have to say, you may even be aware of how they smell. All the information is taken in via your senses and rapidly processed. Tentative conclusions are reached. You decide whether you approve or disapprove, whether you like or dislike, whether you trust or distrust. While you are busy with such things, you are also transmitting and receiving additional visual and verbal behaviours. These give you an opportunity to update your conclusions.

There are five key behaviours involved in establishing rapport:

1 Non-threatening small talk that succeeds in establishing some shared experiences. 'Small talk' greatly aids the process of establishing rapport. The objective is to find something to share before getting down to the real business. The small talk might gently probe for some common experiences. It might be something to do with the weather or with the experiences of travelling to the meeting. The whole idea of small talk is to select a 'safe' topic where it is likely that the other person will have no trouble in meeting you halfway.

2 Appropriate use of the other person's name. Using the other person's name early on in the transaction also helps establish rapport, so long as it isn't inappropriately familiar or done in a routine, 'mechanical' way.

3 Humour. Humour plays an important part. If both you and the other person can find something to laugh about together it paves

the way for a harmonious transaction. A technique for doing this is to make an amusing remark against yourself. It is much too risky at the start of an interaction to make a joke about the other person. Pulling their leg can come later, if and when rapport has been established.

4 Empathy. Empathy is another crucial ingredient when establishing rapport. Empathy is the ability to put yourself in the other person's shoes and see the situation from their point of view. The important thing is to *demonstrate* empathy, not just to feel it.

5 Compatible non-verbal behaviours. Non-verbal behaviours also play a key part. In fact there is evidence to suggest that visual behaviours may be more important than anything else when establishing rapport. There are even techniques for mirroring the other person's non-verbal behaviours for the first few minutes of meeting them, and then testing whether rapport has been established by changing your visual behaviours to see whether the other person will reciprocate by mirroring yours. If this happens, it is an indication that rapport has been established.

Resistance to change

Change invariably triggers some form of human resistance, sometimes subtle, sometimes blatant. It is popular to assume that *other* people resist change but, of course, we are all potential resisters of change. It is always easier to stick to the tried and true than to risk doing something different. This is why people find it difficult to experiment with their own behaviour and to practise using behaviours that are unfamiliar. It is not because, as they'll so often claim, they *can't* do it, but rather that they *won't* do it.

The four most common reasons for resistance to change are:

1 *Parochial self-interest* – People think they will lose something of value as a result. In these cases people focus on their own best interests and not on those of the organization as a whole.

2 *Misunderstanding and lack of trust* – People do not understand its implications and perceive that it might cost them more than they will gain. Misunderstandings and distorted perceptions often

occur when trust is lacking between the initiators of the change
and people on the receiving end of it.

3 *Different assessments* – People assess the situation differently
from the initiators of the change. Managers, for example, often
assume they have all the relevant information required to conduct an adequate assessment of the need for change. They also
tend to assume, conveniently, that those who will be affected by
the change, have the same information. It is rare for either
assumption to be correct. The differences in information inevitably
lead to different assessments.

4 *Low tolerance for change* – People fear that they will not be able
to cope in new, unfamiliar circumstances. Even when people
intellectually accept the need for change, they are sometimes
emotionally unable to make the adjustment. People with a low
tolerance for change therefore tend to fight hard to maintain the
status quo, often without being able to articulate their reasons for
so doing.

There are other reasons for resistance to change. People sometimes
resist change to save face when, for example, they think that supporting change would amount to an admission that some of their
previous decisions or beliefs were wrong. People might also resist
change because of peer group pressure to do so even though, off the
record, they may acknowledge the changes as beneficial.

Strategies for overcoming resistance to change in other people
have to be appropriate to the type of resistance encountered. For
descriptions of the strategies on offer see *Change* on page 29.

So far as overcoming your own tendencies to resist change, it is
best to have some limbering up exercises that you inflict on yourself
from time to time. Do something that you have never done before
at least once each week. It need not be a big thing so long as it is
something novel to you and breaks your normal routine. Travel a
different way to work, visit a part of your organization you are
unfamiliar with, read a different newspaper to your normal one,
drink tea instead of coffee, volunteer to do/lead a project team, etc.
etc. The possibilities are endless and they all do their little bit to
help keep you in a state of readiness for change.

For more detail on change and its associated areas see *Change*,
page 29, *Learning from experience*, page 100, *Self awareness*, page
153, *Self development*, page 154.

Reviewing

Reviewing plays a key part in the process of learning from experience. If you don't review your performance then you have no data to carry forward into an improvement plan (see *Action plans* on page 1). And if you have no improvement plan then you just drift doing things more or less as you have always done them.

The best way to ensure that you review is to adopt a routine that you can swing into either alone or with others. The discipline of the routine makes it more likely that you will review thoroughly enough and not skimp. A simple review procedure is as follows:

1 List what went well and what could have gone better.
2 Select (either from the 'wells' or from the 'betters' or from both) one or two issues to focus upon.
3 Generate ideas on how the selected issues could be tackled in future, either to maintain a success or to improve a weakness.
4 Select a feasible idea or ideas.
5 Plan action so that you are absolutely clear what you have to do.

The joy of this procedure is that it is not laborious. Sometimes the whole process can be completed in five or 10 minutes. It clearly takes longer if you do it with another person or as a group but even then 15 to 20 minutes is adequate unless you are tackling some really contentious issues.

The extraordinary thing is that reviewing isn't done more often as a systematic deliberate process. Most meetings, for example, would benefit by regularly having a 15 minute review as the last item on the agenda. Meetings, despite their reputation for being boring, are rich in opportunities to learn about behaviour but without a review mechanism the opportunities are mostly missed (see *Meetings* on page 106).

For more on the total process of *learning from experience* see page 100.

Rewards

See *Positive reinforcement* on pages 134–136

Rights

A right is something to which you are entitled. The most obvious examples tend to be in the legal sphere (consumers' rights, rights of way, etc) but in addition to rights which are legislated for, you have behavioural rights. Rights are a central issue in being *assertive* (see page 8), since a decision to be assertive, as opposed to aggressive or submissive, is in effect a decision to stand up for your rights in a way that respects other people's rights.

Behavioural rights are more a matter of belief than legislation since they tend to be based on conclusions which you have reached about yourself in relation to others. You may believe, for example, that you have the right to speak your mind and from this will follow certain ways of behaving that will differ markedly from someone who believes they have the right to remain silent. The problem with beliefs is that they can often be unrealistic and stubborn (see *Beliefs* on page 21) but reasonable behavioural rights are such things as:

- the right to express your opinions, views and ideas
- the right to be listened to
- the right to have needs and wants that may differ from other people's
- the right to ask others to respond to your needs and wants
- the right to say no
- the right to express your feelings when you choose to
- the right to be fallible, ie to be wrong and make mistakes sometimes
- the right to be clear what is expected of you
- the right to know how you are doing (feedback)
- the right to know what you need to do to improve
- the right to be consulted about decisions that affect you.

All these rights, reasonable in themselves, become unreasonable if you insist on standing up for them every time they are infringed.

You need to be selective and judge when it is appropriate to assert your rights. Another important implication of behavioural rights such as these, is that if you believe in your own rights then, to be consistent, you must also believe that other people enjoy the same rights. In dealings with other people a balance needs to be struck, therefore, between standing up for your own rights whilst respecting other people's. If, for example, you asked someone not to smoke in your presence (the right to ask others to respond to your needs and wants) you need to respect their right to have different needs and wants and, much more difficult, their right to say no. This then becomes a classic case of conflict resolution (see *Conflict* on page 35).

The clearer you are about your behavioural rights the better prepared you are to handle tricky situations assertively. For more details see *Tricky situations* on page 168 and *Assertiveness* on page 8.

Roles

Roles are characteristic ways of behaving and are especially significant in group and team-work (see *Groups* on page 77 and *Teams* on page 161).

It is vital in carrying out a role to:

- know which behaviours go with which role
- be able to deliver the required mix of behaviours.

Some people know but can't do, others do but don't know. The best of both worlds is to know and do.

Here is a checklist of the key behaviours which comprise the roles of co-ordinator, challenger, doer, thinker and supporter (for an introduction to these roles see *Teams* on page 161).

Co-ordinator role

☞ Co-ordinators employ some or all of the following behaviours. They:

- bring in group members by inviting their comments and soliciting their ideas
- clarify the group's objectives
- 'grasp the nettle' by raising issues and problems that the group ought to face and tackle
- listen to group members' opinions and check that they have been understood
- summarize at frequent intervals
- steer conversations through to consensus decisions by encouraging group members to say what they really think and genuinely agree on a course of action
- 'lead from the front' by deciding what needs to be done in difficult situations, where a consensus cannot be reached or where time is tight.

Challenger role

Challengers employ some or all of the following behaviours. They:

- tend to get their own way by pressurizing people
- have no hesitation in objecting to others' views
- are quite prepared to be a minority of one if they think they are right
- show impatience and irritation with people who are slow on the uptake (they don't suffer fools gladly)
- become exasperated with what they regard as inefficiency
- challenge complacency whenever they come across it
- challenge the 'system' (ie accepted ways of doing things, rules and procedures)
- tend to ginger up people whenever they think they are dragging their feet on something
- tend to point out the snags and difficulties with people's ideas
- they step in and take a positive lead when things aren't progressing well.

Doer role

Doers employ some or all of the following behaviours. They:

- get impatient with people who 'beat about the bush'
- urge people to stick to plans and schedules and meet deadlines

- push ahead and get the job done when things aren't progressing well
- don't mind being unpopular if it gets the job done
- have a reputation for having a no-nonsense 'call a spade a spade' style
- tend to be forceful and dynamic
- press for action to make sure people don't waste time or go round in circles
- urge people to press on with the task in hand especially when they have second thoughts
- like to get straight to the point
- get irritated with flippant people who don't take things seriously enough.

Thinker role

Thinkers employ some or all of the following behaviours. They:

- can be counted on to contribute original ideas
- can quickly see what is wrong with unsound ideas put forward by others
- tend to put forward lots of ideas
- develop other people's ideas so that they are improved
- are careful not to jump to conclusions too quickly
- enjoy analysing situations and weighing up alternatives
- like to anticipate probable difficulties and be prepared for them
- like to ponder alternatives before making up their minds
- have a reputation for being analytical and cautious
- like to think things through before doing something

Supporter role

Supporters employ some or all of the following behaviours. They:

- use humour to ease tensions and maintain good relationships
- avoid getting involved in conflicts
- are always ready to back a good suggestion in the common interest
- tend to change their minds after listening to other people's points of view
- tend to seek approval and support from others

- are friendly and find it easy to establish good rapport with others
- are good at noticing when someone in the group is feeling aggrieved or upset
- work well with a wide range of people
- like to foster good working relationships
- tend to be open about their feelings.

These five roles are complementary. A group or team works best when all the roles are represented. The Co-ordinator ensures that the Challengers and Doers are counterbalanced by the Thinkers and Supporters. A homogeneous group of, say, Challengers is not likely to be very successful. For more on how these roles can be blended into a successful group, see *Groups* on page 77 and *Teams* on page 161.

Seeking ideas

Seeking ideas is a behaviour that doesn't happen all that often. Statistics show that typically it only accounts for two per cent of all the verbal behaviours that take place in a conversation. You are seeking ideas whenever you invite someone else to put forward an idea about a possible course of action. Examples are:

- 'Any ideas?'
- 'We've discussed the problem at length – has anyone any ideas on how to solve the problem?'
- 'How can we improve the situation?'

Seeking ideas is, therefore, a participative behaviour that concentrates on soliciting ideas from other people and does not include proffering one yourself (see *Idea-having* on page 86). Despite the fact that it is one of the rarer species, it is a highly successful behaviour. Eight times out of ten seeking ideas succeeds in eliciting an idea and that is a surprisingly high hit rate.

Seeking ideas is an appropriate behaviour when you want to:

- pick someone else's brains
- encourage a reticent person to come up with ideas
- stop going round in circles

- force someone who is being negative to be more positive
- involve someone in solving a problem so that they have some ownership for the solution.

Self awareness

Despite the fact that it is a basic right to know how you are doing, most people are starved of *feedback* (see page 63) and may even resent it when they get it. In the absence of regular helpful feedback from other people the answer is constantly to subject your own behaviour to scrutiny. The aim in doing this is not to depress yourself but to be open to the possibility of self-improvement.

Here are four suggestions to help you remain aware of your own behaviour and opportunities for its modification and improvement:

1 Whenever you fail to produce desired results, *assume* that the failure resulted from things you did rather than being caused by other factors that were 'beyond your control'. Conduct a careful post-mortem of your own actions and compile a list of all the things you could have done better.

2 Even when you succeed in producing desired results, periodically review your own actions and list what you could have done better. Often you know in your heart of hearts that you are capable of performing better, and your own disappointments with yourself are an important information source.

3 When you are disappointed with the way other people react to you, assume (even though it may not be true) that it is your fault. So when people do not listen to you, do not adopt your suggestion, do not consult you etc, assume that your behaviour was at fault, not theirs. This forces you to scrutinize your own behaviour rather than blame other people.

4 On the rare occasions when people criticize you (see *Criticism* on page 44) and offer you explicit feedback about your behaviour, accept it gratefully rather than springing to your own defence. Feedback is easier to accept if you can do something constructive once you have got it; if you know how to develop yourself, you are more likely to welcome feedback when it is offered and also more likely to solicit it actively. Other people's perceptions of us

are there to be collected if only we can pluck up the courage to ask for them.

Self awareness is a prerequisite for *self development* (see below).

Self development

Self development is the development of yourself, by yourself, through a deliberate process of learning from experience. This definition includes a number of assumptions that are worth expansion.

1 It assumes that it is always possible to develop yourself, not just your outward behaviour but also your inner thought processes and feelings.
2 It assumes that you need to organize it for yourself rather than expecting other people to be responsible for your development.
3 Finally, it assumes that self development needs to be done deliberately rather than left to chance.

For expansion on the first and third assumptions see *Learning from experience* on page 100. The second assumption is the very essence of self development. The argument is that you only have one life, that you are the most important person in the world and that if you don't take responsibility for your own development, who else will? Indeed, who else *can*? Nobody else, no matter how hard they try, can force you to do anything. The door to development is locked with the key on the inside. It is popular to believe that managers are responsible for developing their people but closer examination reveals this to be a nonsense. Managers *are* responsible for providing their people with development opportunities, but it is always up to the individual person to take the opportunities on offer and make something of them.

There are advantages to self development. Since in your life and work you are going to do things anyway, you might as well kill two birds with one stone by doing and learning in parallel. Another advantage is that self development is capable of converting even the most boring situation into a learning opportunity. The philosophy maintains that it is up to you to take initiatives and through so doing to refuse to be bored.

If self development is so wonderful why isn't there more of it about? One of the most common excuses is lack of time. People tend to invest more time deciding on a house purchase or what car to buy than deciding what to do with their lives and how to develop themselves. As John Lennon sang 'Life is what happens to you while you're busy making other plans'. Another deeper-seated inhibition to self development is the avoidance of what is termed 'discomfort anxiety'. This is a strong preference for short term comfort (ie staying with what is familiar) even though it is self-defeating in the long run. An example would be writing a book in longhand instead of learning to use a word processor.

Here is a list of a dozen things that self-developers tend to do:

- Put themselves first (and others a close second)
- Strive to improve their current performance
- Deliberately seek out learning opportunities
- Get learning mileage out of chance events (at work, home, socially)
- Assess own needs
- Set own self-development objectives
- Assess own progress
- Experiment/try new or different things
- Review experiences
- Reach conclusions from experiences
- Plan to implement what has been learned
- Tolerate short term discomfort in the interests of longer term learning.

Skilful behaviour

Skilful behaviour, like any other skill, is acquired through practice. The acid test of a skill is to watch someone else doing something effortlessly and then to try it yourself – you quickly discover that there is much more to it than you imagined. A good example is to watch a skilful presenter, making eye contact with the audience, standing still, using gestures and visual aids to emphasize a point. It looks easy until you try it.

The acquisition of a skill is a tortuous process that takes us through the following sequence:

1 Unconscious incompetence

This is the stage where ignorance is bliss, when it looks easy and you don't realize how much there is to it. The skilful presenter is doing it effortlessly.

2 Conscious incompetence

This is the realization that, when you first try to emulate the skilful performer, you can't do it. This is an umpleasant discovery which may shock you into giving up and returning to the relative comfort of Stage 1.

3 Conscious competence

This stage is hard work! It is where you are able to do a competent presentation but only by investing an enormous amount of conscious effort into every aspect. You have to *force* yourself to make adequate eye contact with the audience and to stand still. You have to force yourself not to talk to the visual aids and to synchronize your gestures with your main messages. This is such hard work that you may decide that it isn't worth the effort and abandon your attempt to acquire the skills in question.

4 Unconscious competence

This stage is the skilful stage when you too can do professional presentations effortlessly! Even this, however, isn't the end of the story because of the very real danger of *complacency* creeping in (see page 35). The more skilful you are, the more you tend to cut corners which, if unchecked for long periods, degenerate into bad habits. The answer is to drop back to conscious competence every now and again to check things out and eradicate the bad habits.

Strokes

If *ego-states* (see page 56) are the backbone of *transactional analysis* (see page 167), strokes are its heartbeat. A stroke is simply a unit of recognition. When someone compliments you ('Well done.' 'That's a good suggestion.' 'You managed that well.' 'I'm glad I talked that through with you.' 'It's always so nice to see you.' 'You have been a great help.') they are giving you a stroke.

In TA it is assumed that we all have stroke quotas, established in early learning. Some need only a few strokes, others need many. Furthermore, all three ego-states, Parent, Adult and Child, have their own stroke requirements. The need for strokes is strong. When a person is not getting their quota, or the right sort of strokes, they go out of their way to manipulate situations in order to obtain the strokes they need. Unfortunately, many of these manoeuvres are counter-productive and 'crooked' and result in *games* (see page 71).

Strokes tell people 'You're OK'. For strokes to function success-fully, however, they need to be genuine rather than phoney and they need to stroke the appropriate ego-state in the other person. It would be no good stroking their Adult, say, if the transaction had largely come from their Child.

The most obvious practical implication of strokes is that we need to help people achieve their stroke quotas. Games and other 'crooked' ways of getting strokes are most prevalent in people who are under their quota.

In TA it is observed that the strokes that work best are often unconditional rather than solely dependent upon someone behav-ing in the desired way. Unconditional strokes come with no strings attached and are given simply because a person is OK with you, warts and all! The vital thing about strokes is not so much in the giving, however, as in the receiving. It is important to observe whether the stroked person accepts or rejects the stroke. If they are feeling 'Not OK' they may reject the stroke by discounting them-selves ('It was nothing really.' 'It didn't take me long.' 'I'm sorry it was so incomplete.'). If what you imagine to be strokes are rejected, they aren't functioning as strokes and need to be replaced by others.

For further advice on how to stroke people authentically see *Praise* on page 135. For other concepts from *transactional analysis* see *Ego-states*, page 56, *Discounts*, page 55, *Games*, page 71, *OKness*, page 123.

Styles

Styles are a convenient way of summarizing a collection of different behaviours under one heading. A style is, therefore, a useful short-hand for various bits and pieces of behaviour that, taken together, give a discernible pattern. Thus we have styles such as autocratic and democratic, each capable of being broken down into its constituent behaviours. Autocratic for example breaks down into:

- lots of telling and little asking
- lots of proposing and little suggesting
- lots of interrupting and little listening
- lots of disagreeing and little building.

Styles are, in effect, *conclusions* we reach about the way others operate. The conclusions are based, as they have to be, on the smaller bits of behaviour that make up a given style. Since styles are so attractively brief there is an understandable temptation to think of all behaviour at a styles-level of description. This leads to two problems:

1 Becoming sloppy in observations of other people's behaviour. Once you have concluded that someone is being autocratic this is likely to become self-reinforcing. In other words, you tend to notice behaviours that confirm the conclusion you have already reached and to ignore the behaviours that contradict it.
2 Intending to adopt a particular style on a particular occasion without realizing that intending is not the same as planning. The 'secret', inasmuch as there is one, is to break style-level descriptions down into smaller behavioural bits. Our behaviour plan can then be built around the 'bits' instead of depending on vague intentions. Intentions are infamous for getting put into action less frequently than plans simply because intentions leave a yawning gap which only plans can bridge. *Intending* to get up early and do two hours work before breakfast is less likely to happen than planning to do it. Planning involves a series of action steps, such as going to bed earlier than usual and setting an alarm (or a failsafe system incorporating two or more alarms!). For more on the need for specificity see *Action plans* on page 1.

Styles of various kinds are described elsewhere in this book. For more detail see *Directive* on page 53, *Consultative* on page 38, *Collaborative* on page 32, *Delegation* on page 49, *Assertiveness* on page 8, *Learning from experience* on page 100.

Submissive behaviour

See *Assertiveness* on pages 8–11

Successes

'Success breeds success' goes the saying in just the same way that behaviour breeds behaviour. After a success it is obviously tempting to relax and bask in feelings of self-congratulation. The advent of the success is so delightful that all thoughts of learning from it are banished. Understandably, therefore, people take success as it comes and rarely consider the ingredients of the success nor how to replicate it.

Learning from successes is just as valid and useful a process as learning from *mistakes* (see page 110). Indeed it could be argued that learning from success is even more useful than learning from mistakes because, by and large, things go right more often than they go wrong. We therefore stand to learn more if we trouble to analyse our successes.

The answer is to develop the habit of asking yourself the question 'What went well?' This forces you to reflect on successes rather than to bask in them. For more on the mechanics of *Learning from experience* see page 100 and *Reviewing* on page 147.

Summarizing

Summarizing is a compact restatement of points which have been made in a discussion. The objective of summarizing is to check on the level of understanding and give an opportunity to sort out misunderstandings.

There are two different ways of accomplishing this objective. The first is, at intervals in the conversation, to give a summary of the salient points as you have understood them. The second is to test understanding by inviting someone else to summarize and check that their summary accords with the one you yourself would have given at that stage in the proceedings. If a number of people are present, invitations to summarize can be shared around rather than becoming the prerogative of one person. This is a splendid incentive for people to listen hard since they never know when they might be called upon to paraphrase what they have heard.

Summarizing reduces ambiguity by pointing things out explicitly and helps to reduce the likelihood that people are agreeing to different things (see *Agreeing* on page 3). Summarizing is a key behaviour in effective meetings where it is usually an important part of the chairing role. In fact, however, any participant in a meeting or discussion has a right to offer a summary to test that their understanding accords with everyone else's. See *Meetings* on page 106.

Suppression

Suppression is a way of hiding your true feelings so that they remain an internal experience but don't manifest themselves in your behaviour. The socialization process trains us to 'have a stiff upper lip' and not express our feelings in an open, straightforward way. As a result some people are already skilled at hiding their feelings behind a behavioural façade. The snag with this is that the suppressed feelings are still experienced internally rather than avoided or prevented. A further difficulty is that repeated mismatching between feelings and behaviour can build up stresses in the system to the extent that something has to 'blow'.

The indiscriminate over-suppression of feelings is generally condemned as unhealthy. When you feel angry, for example, involuntary responses increase your blood pressure, heart rate, rate of breathing, blood flow to the muscles, and metabolism, preparing you for conflict or escape. All systems are go to react angrily and if you don't there is evidence to indicate that repeated suppression eventually leads to furred-up arteries and high blood pressure. The natural physiological mechanisms put us in a state of alert and prepare us for what is called the fight-or-flight response. The problem is that fight-or-flight behaviours are less and less appropriate in today's civilized society and this is how the damage is done.

Healthier alternatives are to learn how to prevent unwanted feelings (see *Preventing unwanted feelings* on page 138) or to practise some form of relaxation or meditation technique (see *Meditation* on page 105).

Synergy
See *Teams* below

Teams

Teams are special. They evolve from *groups* who have learned to work together skilfully (see page 77). A team is a small group (6 to 8 people is a typical size) who co-operate together in such a way that they accomplish more than the sum total of the individuals. The jargon word for this is synergy. This is sometimes expressed as one plus one equals three because you count the 'plus', which represents the interaction between different people, the 'ones'.

The idea that a combination of different people working together can achieve synergy is central to the concept of a team as opposed to a mere group. Eight people each with different views who fail to cohere or who simply proceed by letting the majority view prevail (as in voting) are a group (ie a collection of individuals) not a team.

Research into the differences between successful and unsuccessful teams highlights the importance of having a mix of people with different ways of behaving. It is the *combination* of different roles within a team that seems a crucial factor in its success. A team benefits from the differences rather than the similarities between people. Five key roles are:

- *Co-ordinator* – making sure that objectives are clear and that everyone is involved and committed.
- *Challenger* – questioning ineffectiveness and taking the lead in pressing for improvements/results.
- *Doer* – urging the team to get on with the task in hand.
- *Thinker* – producing carefully considered ideas and weighing up and improving ideas from other people.

- *Supporter* – easing tensions and maintaining harmonious working relationships.

A successful team blends these different roles together so that the
strengths of one compensate for the weaknesses of another. This is
why a mix of *different* people has the potential to dovetail and
become a cohesive team. It is the co-ordinator's job to aid and abet
this dovetailing process. For lists of the specific behaviours that go
with each role see *Roles* on page 149.

There are some characteristics that are helpful in distinguishing a
mere group from a team. Here are eight hallmarks of a team:

- A team has a high success rate, ie more often than not it achieves
what it sets out to do.
- A team agrees clear, challenging objectives, ie everyone in the
team contributes to, shares understanding of, and is committed
to the objectives.
- A team has a co-ordinator (it may not always be the same
person) who adjusts the leadership style along a spectrum, from
participative to autocratic, in the light of circumstances.
- A team has a mix of people who contribute in different but
complementary ways thus achieving synergy, ie the team pro-
duces more than the sum of its individuals.
- A team operates in such a way that a balance is struck between
concern for the task (the 'what') and concern for the process (the
'how').
- A team creates a supportive atmosphere where people are happy
to go at risk, say what they really think, develop one another's
ideas and commit to an agreed course of action even though
there may have been differences of opinion.
- A team learns from experience, both successes and failures, by
reviewing its processes and constantly improving its own performance.
- A team works hard and plays hard, ie its members not only
achieve challenging objectives but enjoy themselves as they do
so.

When a team is functioning at the skilful level and achieving these
eight hallmarks, it alters the behaviour patterns in various ways.
Here are data contrasting behavioural data for a group as opposed
to a team. (For definitions of the *behaviour categories* see page 26.)

Behaviour category	Frequency with which each behaviour occurs in a group (percentages)	Frequency with which each behaviour occurs in a team (percentages)
Seeking ideas	2	6
Proposing	13	8
Suggesting	7	10
Building	3	8
Disagreeing	6	2
Supporting	14	15
Difficulty stating	11	7
Seeking clarification/ information	15	20
Clarifying/explaining/ informing	29	24

The striking differences are that a team increases seeking ideas, suggesting, building and seeking clarification and decreases proposing, disagreeing, difficulty stating and clarifying/explaining/informing. Supporting stays about the same but there is a marked difference in quality which is not reflected in the figures. In a group there is more acquiescing and in a team there is more commitment (see *Agreeing* on page 3).

It is easy to assume that teams are 'a good thing' and therefore, in some way, essential, but experience indicates that they are only essential in certain sorts of situations.

The simplest way to decide whether a collection of individuals (a group) will be sufficient or whether a genuine team operating at the skilful stage is necessary, is to look at the nature of the task to be tackled.

If the task is *certain*, there is less need to share and a group will suffice. As the uncertainty of the task increases there is more need to share and a team is necessary. Suppose, for example, a group is given a task that is tightly defined and where the group has previous experience of similar tasks, it is likely to succeed by operating at a formal stage level. If, however, a group is set an ambiguous task with an uncertain outcome and with little previous experience to draw on it is unlikely to succeed unless it operates as a team at the skilful level. Clearly, the more prescribed the task the less room for manoeuvre and the less of a challenge for the group. On the other hand, tasks that are dogged with uncertainty are more of a challenge and put greater onus on the co-operative skills of the team members.

This is an important distinction because it reminds us that a high level of teamwork, whilst perfectly desirable, is not absolutely essential for many routine activities. Teamwork is vital for the tougher, more challenging activities which, whilst less frequent, are more crucial when they do occur.

Telephone behaviour

The telephone as an instrument of communication between people is being used more and more. Some of the reasons for this are:

- Telephoning is often more convenient than travelling to meet people face-to-face.
- Telephoning saves time, both because telephone conversations tend to be shorter than face-to-face conversations and because it is not necessary to spend time travelling.
- Telephoning is cheaper than face-to-face meeting, mainly because of savings on travelling expenses. This is dramatically true with telephone calls overseas.

As a result of this, more people than ever before are telephone users.

The growing popularity of the telephone is not, however, without its problems. The more people have access to the telephone, the more likely it is that you will encounter unskilled telephone users. Whenever this happens, the onus is on you to control the call and steer the conversation to a successful conclusion. This, in essence, is what telephone behaviour is all about.

Whenever you have dealings with someone face-to-face you can see them. Upon meeting them you instantly see what they look like, and quickly observe their facial expressions, gestures and body language. In addition you can hear what they say and how they say it. So if you are sufficiently observant, you have lots of information about them. This is important because you reach judgements and conclusions about everyone you meet based, first and foremost, on these observations of their behaviour.

By contrast, whenever you have dealings with someone over the telephone you cannot *see* them. This simple fact deprives you of most of the information you would normally have about the other person. You are therefore obliged to base your judgements and conclusions about them on what you hear them say and how they say it.

The fact that you can only hear behaviour on the telephone has both advantages and disadvantages. Some of the disadvantages are:

- It is more difficult to establish rapport on the telephone. In face-to-face meetings all the visual signals are a great aid to getting on the same wavelength with someone. Without them this is tougher to accomplish.
- When you telephone someone you are more likely to intrude at an inconvenient time and not realize it. When you meet someone you can see whether it is convenient or inconvenient and act accordingly.
- The telephone increases the likelihood of jumping to the wrong conclusions. It is easier, for example, to conclude that someone is being abrupt if you only have what they say and how they say it to go on. It is also easier to assume that you have someone's undivided attention when you talk to them on the 'phone.
- When you are having a telephone conversation you are more likely to be distracted and let your attention wander. You don't suddenly go blind for the duration of a 'phone call and are, therefore, prey to all sorts of visual distractions – people walking past the window, someone coming in to see you and so on. You are also more likely to be tempted into doing two (or even more than two) things at once. You know the caller can't see you continuing to sign letters, do the crossword, read a magazine, pull faces at a colleague . . .
- On the telephone it is more difficult to communicate accurate information and avoid misunderstandings. People remember more of what they see than what they hear. On the telephone, all information has to be transmitted in words and that limitation increases communication problems.

On the other hand the telephone has some advantages:

- On balance it is easier to reach someone by telephoning them than by trying to see them. Not only is it more convenient to pick up the 'phone and make contact, you are also more likely to succeed since few people are able to ignore the telephone and leave it unanswered.

- When you speak to someone on the telephone it is easier for you to represent your company or organization. As far as the person on the other end is concerned you *are* the company or organization. The fact that they can't see you increases your authority in their eyes.

- Telephone conversations are, on average, significantly shorter than face-to-face conversations. The telephone, therefore, saves time and gives you the opportunity to be more businesslike, if that is appropriate.

- Since telephone conversations are usually confined to you and just one other person, not a group of people, it is easier to take initiatives and control the conversation. This is a relative point. No-one is claiming it is easy to control the conversation, just that with some simple, learnable techniques it is easier on the telephone than in the more complex circumstances of face-to-face meetings.

- On the telephone it is easier (though not necessarily easy) to be firm, to say what you might not have the courage to say face-to-face. This 'Dutch courage' can be useful if you are in a situation that requires you to be resolute.

The key to minimizing the disadvantages and reaping the advantages of communications over the telephone is the way you behave. Here is a list of specific standards to aim for:

- Answer the telephone promptly – within three rings if possible.
- Start each telephone call by saying who you are, your name and position.
- Always enquire whether or not it is convenient to proceed.
- If an incoming call is not convenient, explain why and take the name and number of the caller and offer to phone back.
- Explain, in a straightforward way, the purpose of the telephone call.
- Establish and use the other person's name early in the telephone conversation.
- Ask open questions.

- Listen, resist the temptation to interrupt.
- When listening demonstrate that you are by making 'continuity noises' such as 'um', 'yes', 'really'.
- Concentrate – don't be tempted to do two things at once. Give the telephone conversation your undivided attention.
- Make notes and 'read back' key points so that the caller knows you are being attentive.
- Be lavish in explaining what you are doing – especially if it involves a silence while the caller 'hangs on'.
- Err on the side of being helpful – volunteer help, don't wait to be asked.
- Use assertive behaviour (see *Assertiveness* on page 8) to control the call. Stay assertive even when you don't feel like it and *especially* when dealing with a submissive or aggressive person.
- Finish by recapping exactly what it is you are going to do as a result of the telephone conversation.
- Smile, for even though you can't be seen by the other person, if you smile it helps your voice to sound more assertive and friendly.

Always remember, behaviour breeds behaviour and that, so far as the person on the other end of the telephone is concerned, *you are what you say*!

Testing understanding
See *Summarizing* on pages 159–160

Transactional analysis

Transactional analysis (TA) is the name given to a number of related concepts that seek to throw light on the way people behave and feel.

The basic assumptions in TA are that:

- people learn at an early age ways of feeling and behaving that tend to become habitual regardless of their continued appropriateness.
- feelings *cause* behaviour.

- even though characteristic ways of feeling and behaving are habitual, they can be controlled and, if necessary, unproductive ways of feeling and behaving can be replaced with more satisfactory ones.
- you can do much to help other people, whether they be your superiors, associates, colleagues or subordinates, to modify their feelings and behaviour for better.
- feelings of doubt, indecision, embarrassment, fear and anger drain energy from both individuals and organizations and, in various ways, exact a heavy toll in time and money.

TA claims to be a simple and practical method for understanding and modifying human behaviour. It is intended to give you some comprehensible concepts so that you can improve yourself and help others to do the same. This process is not intended to be dangerous or impossible, or to require the help of experts.

The basic TA concepts together with their implications are given in the following sections (best read in this sequence): *Ego-states*, page 56, *Strokes*, page 156, *Discounts*, page 55, *Games*, page 71, *OKness*, page 123.

Tricky situations

Some situations are tougher than others. The trickier the situation the more your behaviour matters as a means of influencing the other person or people.

There are three factors which tend to make a situation especially testing. If any one of them applies then that is tough enough. If they all apply, then that makes the situation even harder to handle successfully.

- The first factor is time. The less you have of it as, for example, in a short face-to-face contact, the more difficult it is to impress and/or influence. Every door to door salesman knows that.
- A second factor relates to objectives. When the people involved in the interaction have *conflicting* objectives it is more difficult to reach agreement. Every negotiator has experience of that.
- Thirdly, when the situation is emotionally charged with feelings

running high, it is more difficult to resolve. Every husband or wife in the middle of a row knows that.

The only hope in a tricky situation is to look to your behaviour and use it to influence the behaviour of others for the better. The secret of success is to use your Adult (see *Ego-states* on page 56 and hang on to assertive behaviour (see *Assertiveness* on page 8 and *Conflict* on page 35).

Triggers

A trigger is any event which causes a behavioural reaction. Literally, *any* event can act as a trigger. It may be a spoken remark from someone or just a 'meaningful' look. It may be a place, or a time of day or a specific occurrence, such as being stuck in a traffic jam or being promoted.

Triggers are important because they help us understand why people behave as they do. Behaviour is always a reaction to a trigger of some kind. Scratching, for example, is a reaction to an itch. Answering a question is a reaction to having been asked a question. Going on the defensive is a reaction to criticism. And so on.

Identifying the triggers or cues for your own behaviour and other people's provides a useful foothold when it comes to working out how to change or modify behaviour. See *Behaviour modification* on page 16.

Unhelpful behaviour

Unhelpful behaviours are those which hinder you from achieving your objective and/or which run the risk of giving other people a bad impression of you. Obviously what is helpful and what is unhelpful depends to a large extent on the circumstances of the situation. Nonetheless, there are certain behaviours that tend to engender unfavourable reactions in the people you have dealings with. Here is a list of 19 such behaviours:

- Lean away from the other person with hands clenched, arms crossed and legs crossed.
- Look at the other person for less than 50 per cent of the time.
- Listen silently with no continuity noises and/or interrupt before the other person has had their say.
- Have a blank expression.
- Sit opposite the other person (rather than beside them).
- Don't use the other person's name or use it artificially so that it jars.
- Don't ask questions or ask closed questions.
- Offer no summaries and don't check your understanding.
- Stick rigidly to saying things that are routine and standard.
- Don't acknowledge the other person's expressed feelings or point of view.
- Acquiesce or never explicitly agree with the other person.
- Pick holes in the other person's ideas.
- Criticize the other person.
- Disagree first then say why.
- Be defensive and never admit to any inadequacy.
- Be secretive and withhold information from the other person even though it affects them.
- Have visual and verbal behaviours out of step with each other.
- Remain aloof and don't touch the other person.
- Don't give the other person anything.

That's the bad news. For the good news see *Helpful behaviour* on page 84.

Verbal behaviour

Verbal behaviour covers everything you say to people either face-to-face or on the telephone. This clearly covers such a vast range of possibilities that it is best to break verbal behaviour down into a number of categories and concentrate on some specifics. Nine such categories are introduced and defined on page 27.

Obviously what you say to another person and the way you say it will have an effect on what they say back as a response. The 'chemistry' of different verbal behaviours in interaction with one another has been carefully investigated and here are some of the findings together with their implications for you.

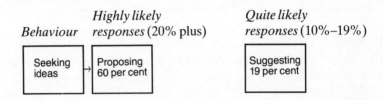

Seeking ideas is a powerful behaviour. Nine times out of ten it is successful in provoking some ideas from the other person. It is a helpful behaviour to use whenever you need to pick someone else's brains.

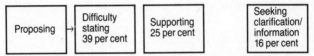

Proposing ideas unfortunately provokes difficulties or objections more often than it wins support. If you want to 'flush out' people's reservations then proposing is a good behaviour to use. If, on the other hand, you want to make it more likely that there will be agreement to your idea then the next behaviour is a safer bet.

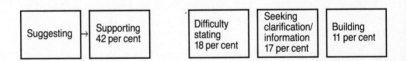

Suggesting ideas is a more effective way of gaining agreement than proposing ideas. There are, of course, no guarantees that it will succeed because your idea may be such a rotten one that even though it is suggested it runs into difficulties. The actual statistics reveal that four times out of ten a suggestion is followed by an agreement and that isn't a bad hit rate.

| Building | → | Seeking clarification/ information 36 per cent | Supporting 32 per cent | | Building 15 per cent | Difficulty stating 11 per cent |

Building on someone else's idea is a powerful way to get their wholehearted support. Despite this, building is a fairly rare behaviour. It seems that people find it easier to find fault with ideas than to build them up into something better. This is a good example of having a choice. People who think about their behaviour are more likely to try building than people who are in the habit of immediately criticizing ideas. The fact that seeking clarification is so prevalent reminds us what a potentially confusing behaviour building can be. The lesson is to 'flag' building so that people are in no doubt, and then supporting and more building are the most likely reactions.

| Disagreeing | → | Clarifying/ explaining/ informing 42 per cent | Disagreeing 31 per cent | | Seeking clarification/ information 10 per cent |

Disagreeing on seven out of ten occasions triggers a defensive reaction or even further disagreements. It is interesting how often people get locked into a disagreeing 'spiral' where one disagreement breeds another which, in turn, breeds another and so on. Disagreeing is very much a last resort. It is best to try some of the more constructive options first.

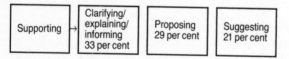

| Supporting | → | Clarifying/ explaining/ informing 33 per cent | Proposing 29 per cent | Suggesting 21 per cent |

Agreeing with something someone else has said is a powerful way to encourage them to go on and say more. Eight times out of ten this will be the effect. Agreeing is, therefore, a useful behaviour if you want to gain more information from the other person. It isn't an appropriate behaviour if you want them to shut up.

Difficulty stating	→

Clarifying/ explaining/ informing 18 per cent	Proposing 17 per cent	Disagreeing 15 per cent
Seeking clarification/ information 12 per cent	Seeking ideas 11 per cent	Suggesting 10 per cent

Pointing out difficulties is a very common behaviour but is one of the riskier ones because research shows that it is far from certain how people will take it. Marginally, the most likely reaction is to offer some clarification or explanation. However, people often take umbrage and start disagreeing or, if you persist with difficulties, they may give up and go and find someone more positive to talk to. You need to watch carefully to see whether pointing out difficulties is hindering or helping the proceedings.

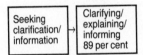

Seeking clarification/ information	→	Clarifying/ explaining/ informing 89 per cent

No surprises here. If you ask for clarification then nine times out of ten you will get it. Seeking clarification is a frequent behaviour that exerts a powerful influence over the behaviour of the other person. It is a very useful behaviour when trying to get to the bottom of things and when you need to tease information out of the other person.

Clarifying/ explaining/ informing	→	Clarifying/ explaining/ informing 42 per cent	Seeking clarification 31 per cent	Difficulty stating 15 per cent	Supporting 10 per cent

Informing is the behaviour that happens more often than any other in conversation between people. This isn't surprising, of course, since the overall purpose of talking with someone is to impart information of some kind. The most interesting aspect is how informing breeds informing, which breeds informing and so on, in what can be a time-consuming loop. Sometimes this is appropriate and necessary. At other times the loop amounts to going round in circles and not getting anywhere fast.

The reason why people often prolong the informing loop is because it is a relatively 'safe' way to pass the time. When you offer a piece of information, you don't commit yourself in quite the same way that you do when you propose or suggest an idea.

The lesson from all this? Simply that the behaviours you use have known shaping effects on the behaviours you get back from other people. The data underline the fact that you are more likely to succeed with people if you think about your behaviour and select and use behaviours that help rather than hinder progress towards your objective. This process is enhanced still further if you adopt visual behaviours which reinforce the things you are saying. It is the combination of verbal and visual that has the desired effect. For guidance on *non-verbal behaviours* see page 116.

Win-win

Win-win describes one of three possible outcomes from a transaction between people. The other two are lose-lose and win-lose. A win-win outcome is where all parties involved are successful in achieving their objectives. Clearly this is most difficult to achieve when people's objectives are in conflict, but even then, with skill, a win-win can be secured.

The key behaviours that, even in the most difficult circumstance, make a win-win outcome more likely are:

- being open about your objective, what you hope to achieve
- encouraging the other people involved to reciprocate by being equally open about their objectives
- exploring different objectives for common ground
- suggesting common objectives in an even-handed way, ie that favour what they want to achieve at least as much as what you want to achieve.

In addition the eight key behaviours typical of successful negotiators (see *Negotiating* on page 113) are all relevant to achieving a win-win outcome.

Here is an example of win-win behaviour overheard, coincidentally whilst writing this section, as my four-year-old son, James, played with a friend.

James: 'I'm the leader.'
Mark: 'No. I'm the leader.'
James: 'I want to be the leader.'
Mark: 'No. You said I could be the leader.'
  pause
James: 'I know! Let's *both* be the leader.'
Mark: 'How could we do that?'
James: 'You be the leader in front and I'll be the leader behind.'
Mark: 'OK.'

Worry

Worry is an unwanted feeling that frequently spills over into behaviour. Fortunately worry is a preventable feeling but it is vital to read the section on *Preventing unwanted feelings* (on page 138) before reading the remainder of this section because what follows assumes you have understood the two options involved.

Unproductive worry hinders your behaviour in a variety of ways. All or some of the following might apply to you:

- You can't settle to anything. You flit butterfly-like from one activity to the next.
- You overeat, smoke, drink, bite your nails etc.
- You don't give your best.
- You become tense, short-tempered and irritable with other people.
- You procrastinate.
- You become accident prone.
- You sleep badly.
- You become physically ill (ie get ulcers, headaches, tummy upsets).

Your worry is always triggered by some external event or happening. Typical examples might be when:

- thinking about gloomy things over which you have no direct control (ie the economy, wars, famine, natural disasters, getting older, dying).
- people close to you engage in dangerous/risky activities (eg mountaineering, riding a motorcycle, flying).
- you are waiting (eg for someone overdue to come home, to go into the dentist).
- before going to any big event where you are not sure you will be able to cope (eg to an interview, to a meeting, to a party, to an exam).
- you have pains in the chest, lumps in your breast, shortage of breath etc.
- you do something new/unfamiliar.

Clearly, ideas for changing the events that trigger your worry will depend on the exact circumstances, but here are some thought-starters that might help you to arrive at a feasible plan:

- Keep a worry log and when you have found out what worries you, plan to avoid it.
- Keep a list of things you worry about and analyse it from time to time to see what your worrying changed.
- Plan your day so that you have too much to do. Being busy is one of the best antidotes to worry.
- Cut down your waiting time or if this isn't possible keep busy while you wait.
- Each time you start to worry say to yourself 'What action can I take *right now* to alleviate my fears?' If you can think of something do it. If you can't think of anything at least realize the futility of your worrying.
- Deliberately force yourself to do something you worried about. You will find it isn't nearly so bad as you expected!
- Allocate a specific time each day as your 'worry time'. You'll find it extraordinarily difficult to find anything to worry about.

Rather than modify anything to do with the external events that trigger your worry you might decide to go for option 2 and identify the thoughts or beliefs that herald your worry and examine them for possible replacements. Typical thoughts for feelings of worry are:

- Wouldn't it be *terrible* if such and such happened?
- I'm sure they have met with an accident.
- I fear the worst. It's sure to crash.
- I know I won't be able to cope.
- I'm sure I have got cancer/heart disease.
- It's only natural to worry.
- I care, so I worry.

And, finally, here are some thought-starters on ways of replacing unrealistic thoughts and beliefs that provoke feelings of worry so that they become more realistic and less likely to hinder your behaviour:

- Worrying doesn't change anything.
- What action can I take *right now*?
- In 100 years time my worries will be of no consequence.
- What is the *worst possible* thing that could happen? What is the likelihood?
- No news is good news!
- Nothing can *make* me worry. I choose to worry!
- Why worry?

Further best-selling management books from IPM

20 Ways to Manage Better
Andrew Leigh

An invaluable distillation of management wisdom which deserves a place on every manager's desk.

The book has 20 short chapters, each on a different topic, which the busy manager can use to improve his or her performance. They include: setting objectives, coaching, problem people, controlling your time, meetings, negotiating, better reading and listening, recruitment and selection.

'The author grabs your attention at the opening of each chapter and whisks you through to the closing sentence quite painlessly. But en route he has given you plenty to think about, and more importantly, plenty to put into operation in your office tomorrow.'

The Director

0 85292 334 1

Management Methods
Derek Torrington, Jane Weightman and Kirsty Johns

Management Methods is a handbook for the busy manager who doesn't have time to read many management books. It follows a unique 'dip-in' format with 50 action plans covering many different situations and concise explanations of why the relevant methods should work, as well as how to work them. The plans deal with a wide range of management activities, from report-writing to organizational politics, from the subtleties of counselling to the precision of statistical sampling. All the units are self-contained, making the book especially convenient to browse through on trains, at airports, at home, or to use when preparing for a meeting.

'a really useful book, the sort of book you would actually wish to buy and have with you when doing things.'

The Times Higher Educational Supplement

0 85292 355 4

Everyone Needs a Mentor
How to foster talent within the organization
David Clutterbuck

Mentoring promises to be the management development technique of the future. Generations of new young employees have learned the company ropes, developed their experience and confidence and progressed up the career ladder under the watchful guidance of more experienced managers. The well-known writer and journalist, David Clutterbuck explains the formalization of this process and explores all aspects of mentoring.

'Anyone involved in training and staff development cannot afford to ignore this innovative means of fostering talent.'
Management Services

0 85292 345 7

Staff Appraisal
A first step to effective leadership
Gerry Randell, Peter Packard and John Slater

This completely revised and updated edition presents an analytical approach to the skills of staff appraisal and advocates training techniques to improve managers' ability to monitor their subordinates' performance and develop their potential.

The book successfully combines academic analysis with industrial relevance to produce an extremely readable book for all those who want to improve their management and leadership skills.

0 85292 333 3

Creating a Committed Workforce
Peter Martin and John Nicholls

Learn the lessons of the British success stories of the 1980s!

How have major companies achieved dramatic improvements in productivity and results? In this perceptive and hard hitting study, the authors go behind the scenes and talk to the leaders in 14 pioneering businesses like Jaguar and Raleigh, Burton and Schweppes. Here they find profound changes – such as profit-sharing, systematic disclosure of information, flatter management structures, worker accountability for quality and moves towards 'single status' – are commonplace. Such changes reflect the impact of Japanese and American management; they are also laying the foundations for the resurgence of UK industry and commerce.

0 85292 379 1

The Institute of Personnel Management is one of the leading publishers of books for personnel professionals, general managers and students. For further information on the full range of IPM titles please contact

The Publications Department
The Institute of Personnel Management
IPM House
Camp Road
London SW19 4UX
Tel: (081) 946 9100